D1566846

Better Homes and Gardens®

Your Child
THE LATCHKEY YEARS

BETTER HOMES AND GARDENS® BOOKS

Editor: Gerald M. Knox
Art Director: Ernest Shelton
Managing Editor: David A. Kirchner
Department Head, Food and Family Life: Sharyl Heiken

President, Book Group: Jeramy Lanigan
Vice President, Retail Marketing: Jamie L. Martin
Vice President, Administrative Services: Rick Rundall

BETTER HOMES AND GARDENS® MAGAZINE
President, Magazine Group: James A. Autry
Editorial Director: Doris Eby

MEREDITH CORPORATION OFFICERS
Chairman of the Executive Committee: E. T. Meredith III
Chairman of the Board: Robert A. Burnett
President: Jack D. Rehm

YOUR CHILD: THE LATCHKEY YEARS
Editor: Elizabeth Woolever
Contributing Editor: Mary Kay Shanley
Editorial Project Manager: Liz Anderson
Graphic Designer: Mary Schlueter Bendgen
Electronic Text Processor: Paula Forest
Contributing Photographer: Jim Kascoutas
Contributing Illustrator: Buck Jones

The booklet shown on page 38, *When School's Out and Nobody's Home*, is available from the National Committee for Prevention of Child Abuse, Attn: Publications BHG, 332 S. Michigan Ave., Suite 1600, Chicago, IL 60604-4357.

Learning to stay home alone is a major milestone in your youngster's journey toward independence. It's a milestone in your life as well. Allowing your child to become a "latchkey kid" indicates that you feel your youngster is maturing into a responsible young person. But deciding that your youngster is capable of staying home alone is only the beginning. The transition from day care or a baby-sitter to being home alone—even for part of the day—requires much preparation. By sharing feelings, understanding responsibilities, and anticipating problems before they crop up, you and your child can enjoy a positive experience.

The first part of this book is filled with no-nonsense suggestions to help you guide your youngster into the new role. The last part of the book is written for your child. It looks at the latchkey years from a kid's point of view, providing guidelines as well as fill-in-the-blank pages to help make decisions when they are on their own.

THE LATCHKEY-CHILD SITUATION

In the not-too-distant past, most youngsters were welcomed home from school with a glass of milk, a plate of cookies, and Mother. But today many children let themselves into an empty house after school and fix their own plate of cookies and milk. They're called "latchkey kids" because they often wear a house key on a string or chain around their necks.

More than six million children in this country spend part of every day alone. Besides being alone after school, many youngsters get themselves off to school in the morning after Mom and Dad already have left for work.

Latchkey kids are far more common today than they were even a few years ago, because more and more mothers are entering the work force. The "traditional" household with a working father and a mother who stays home with the children is certainly no longer the norm.

Early elementary-age youngsters in dual-income families still require before- and after-school supervision. Often, older siblings hold part-time jobs or are involved in extracurricular activities at school so they aren't around to care for little brothers and sisters. Furthermore, because our society is so mobile, grandparents or perhaps a favorite aunt and uncle are not as likely to live close enough to care for the youngster. That means parents must search for an alternative, such as a drop-in day-care center, a program operated at school, or a baby-sitter.

Eventually, however, youngsters outgrow the need for such supervision. As a maturing child's sense of responsibility develops, the possibility of caring for oneself starts to look more and more attractive.

At what age do most youngsters begin the latchkey years? There's no single answer. And research on the subject is scanty. Some children are left alone as early as age 6, a practice not endorsed by child-care authorities. Six-year-olds are not mature enough to make responsible decisions about their own welfare. (In many states, it's illegal to leave a child under a certain age home alone.) Many experts say the earliest age at which it's OK to leave a child unsupervised is 10. Others say 12, while still others say 14. But the fact is that you and your child are best able to judge when the child is sufficiently responsible to take care of him- or herself.

The Importance Of the Decision

Allowing your youngster to become a latchkey kid is not as simple as saying, "I think you're old enough to stay home alone for a couple of hours every day. We'll start next week."

True, once the youngster is old enough to stay alone, the latchkey-kid situation may appear on the surface to be beneficial to everyone: You'll save on child-care costs, and your youngster may jump at the opportunity to be "independent."

But it's actually much more involved. So, you owe it to yourself *and* your child to think about both the pros and cons of having a child home alone. You want to do

THE LATCHKEY-CHILD SITUATION

everything you can to guarantee the best experience for yourself and your child.

This chapter will help you look at both the benefits and the risks. It will help you and your youngster decide together whether the latchkey-kid route is best for your family. If you decide it is the best route, the rest of this book will help you get ready for the new arrangement.

The Benefits

Enjoying independence. For the youngster following a regimented program all day at school, staying alone can provide a cherished feeling of independence. During the school day, students are told where to sit, what to study, and when to eat lunch. All their actions are dictated by the school. After that, many children welcome the chance to be on their own for a while.

An opportunity to mature. Youngsters who stay alone learn to make decisions for themselves and, consequently, take responsibility for their own actions. As their problem-solving skills develop, they are better able to prevent possible problems. And success at problem solving helps a youngster feel more competent, an invaluable component of self-esteem.

Developing skills. Out of necessity or desire, latchkey kids often develop more domestic skills—especially in the kitchen—than their counterparts who stay with an adult after school. Generally, parents depend on the youngster to help more around the house, too.

The Risks

The emotional issue. How does the youngster feel about staying alone? Excited? Rejected? Cautious? Deserted? Resentful? Angry? Afraid? Some youngsters jump at the chance to enjoy some peace and quiet at home after a day crammed with activity at school. Others spend the school day dreading the silence of an empty home.

Obviously, a child's emotional response to staying alone varies according to the child. But research indicates that fear is the most common negative feeling, especially in the winter when darkness comes early.

Another common feeling is loneliness, probably because latchkey kids are frequently required to stay inside or play alone in the yard until a parent gets home.

The safety issue. How safe are latchkey kids? Youngsters are not mentally or emotionally equipped to handle emergency situations, such as fire, accidents, or illness, as well as adults. In major cities, for instance, one in every six calls received by fire departments involves a child or children alone at home. Poison control centers report similar situations.

Furthermore, youngsters home alone who have not been taught good survival skills may be more likely to fall victim to strangers. Although rape, attack, and theft are rare, they do occur. (For information on teaching a child to deal with strangers, see "The Rules of the House" on pages 22–31.)

The school issue. Does a youngster who's unsupervised after school ever get around to doing homework? Often, the answer is no. That may be OK, if there's time to do the homework after supper. On the other hand, it can be an organizational problem for youngsters who are busy in the evening or who have early bedtimes.

Another problem is that parents may never see notes sent home by the teacher. That, however, tends to be a concern whether the child goes home to an empty house or heads for a day-care center or baby-sitter's home. (Some schools send the principal's newsletter in the mail because, it seems, *no* youngster is able to get it into parents' hands.)

Also, teachers say some latchkey kids have difficulty socializing because they spend so much time alone.

Preparing for the Decision

Obviously, it's ideal if you and your child have a choice between a day-care center or baby-sitter *or* staying at home alone. For economic reasons, not everyone has an option. If you have a choice, the switch to staying alone most likely will occur when your youngster is in the upper elementary grades.

Sometimes, it's the youngster who first asks, "When will I be old enough to stay home alone?" Or, you might be the one who initiates the discussion by asking your child, "How would you feel about staying home alone part of the day?" Either way, the time is probably right to discuss having your youngster become a latchkey kid.

Is your youngster ready? You may know several youngsters younger than your child who already stay alone before school, after school, or both. Chances are, you also know some children older than your youngster who still do not stay home by themselves.

That's because becoming a latchkey kid is an individual matter, not one arbitrarily determined by age.

Think back. Not every youngster walks by age 10 months. Not every kid rides a bicycle by age 6. Not every child reads in first grade. Children mature physically, emotionally, socially, and academically at different ages.

Your job is to decide whether your youngster is mature enough to handle the responsibilities of staying alone. What other children do shouldn't matter.

Guidelines for Deciding

To decide whether or not your child can stay home alone, ask yourself these questions. Since each child and situation is different, weigh all the answers to make a decision for your family.

- Is your child mature enough to handle the responsibilities of being on her own?
- Does your youngster adapt to new situations as well as most children his age?
- Is your youngster afraid of the dark?
- Does your youngster generally observe your household rules?
- Does your child depend on you to solve most problems or does she try to think matters through herself?
- When a problem arises requiring adult assistance, does your child seek help?
- Does your youngster find useful and interesting activities to do by himself?
- If you ask your youngster to do chores, does she get them done without a lot of coaxing or supervision?
- Does your youngster share daily activities and happenings—both good and bad—with you?
- Do you and your child communicate your feelings well?
- Does your youngster accept your reasons for leaving him alone?
- Does your child let you know where she is going before leaving the house?
- How does the youngster get along with his sisters and brothers?
- Can your youngster communicate adequately with other adults, such as the neighbors?
- How promptly does your child finish homework? Is the youngster's work accurate and complete?
- Does your youngster consistently get ready for school or day care on time?
- Have you left your youngster home alone for short periods of time? If so, how did she handle the situation?
- If your child has been with a baby-sitter or in a day care, does he express an interest in spending more time alone?

There's no clear-cut path to follow in deciding whether your youngster is ready to stay alone. But generally speaking, the child should handle responsibility well, follow directions, use good judgment, and feel good about being home alone. (See "Guidelines for Deciding" on page 7.) If you must monitor your child's actions constantly while you're home, the child probably won't function well independently when you're not around. On the other hand, if your child seems fairly independent and responsible when you're around, the youngster may be ready to stay alone.

If your child wants to try staying alone, but you aren't sure, speak with the youngster's teacher, baby-sitter, or day-care director. These people spend a lot of time with your youngster and can help assess the child's maturity level.

Are you ready? Just because your child wants to stay home alone doesn't mean you're ready to let that happen. You, as well as your child, must feel comfortable about the arrangement, so deal with your own feelings before any changes are made.

For starters, if the thought of having your youngster home alone sends you into a panic, you'll be better off leaving the child at the baby-sitter's house or at the day-care center awhile longer. If you will worry at work about what's going on at home, you won't be an effective employee.

Likewise, if leaving your child home alone makes you feel guilty, you may want to postpone any changes for a while. When you begin thinking positively about your child staying home alone, those gushes of guilt will subside. Then, you'll be ready to let go.

Abandonment vs. A Learning Situation

Besides affecting your own peace of mind, your attitude about the latchkey-kid arrangement greatly affects your child. If you feel like you're abandoning your child, the youngster is likely to feel abandoned. On the other hand, if you have a positive attitude, the situation can be a learning opportunity for your youngster.

Offering an explanation. If you initiated the idea of your child staying home alone, explain your reasons for the change. If your youngster thinks you're taking the latchkey route just to save money—and that other considerations don't matter—it may make the child feel guilty if she doesn't want to stay home alone. Or it may cause her to worry unduly about family finances.

A main reason for starting the latchkey-kid arrangement probably will be that both parents are working and other arrangements are not possible or desirable. But don't let your youngster feel responsible if you're no longer able to find suitable day care. And latchkey kids shouldn't feel responsible for making their parents work.

During your discussions, make sure your youngster understands why you work in the first place. Failing to share your reasons can lead to an upsetting conclusion on your child's part: You work so you don't have to stay at home with your child.

To help your youngster understand your work situation, take him to your workplace to show him where you are employed. You already may have done this before the child entered day care or while he was in day care. But a repeat trip will help your youngster visualize where you go each day. As much as possible, show your child what you do at work.

The telephone will be a vital link between the two of you, so show the child where the phone is located in comparison to your workstation. If your job makes it difficult to come to the phone, explain how you'll get a message if the child calls you.

Finally, if your job is a long way from your home, point that out. The concept of distance is important. If your youngster encounters an emergency at home, it's vital for her to understand that you can't be there immediately.

Making the Decision

Once you've looked at the situation from all angles, make out a list of pros and cons about having a latchkey kid. Ask your child to do the same. When both lists are complete, take one point from your list and discuss it. Then discuss one point from your child's list. Continue until you've talked about all items on both lists.

Encourage your youngster to discuss the arrangement by asking questions:

"How do you feel about staying alone?"

"What do you think is the most exciting thing about staying home alone?"

"What do you think is the worst thing about staying home alone?"

Don't dwell on the negative, but don't suppress it, either. Let your child know that it's OK to have concerns and fears. If you talk over those concerns together, you'll be surprised at the excellent conclusions you'll reach. Also, by considering "what if" questions, you may avoid problems later.

You and your youngster both may decide she's ready to try staying home alone, but making the decision is just the first step. The rest of this book will help you prepare for the change.

However, if your youngster decides he doesn't want to stay home alone yet, let him know the decision is OK. You can discuss it again in six months or so.

On the other hand, if *you* don't feel your youngster should stay home alone, explain your reasons. Remember, even if your child disagrees with your decision, you are the parent and you are in charge.

If it doesn't work out. Sometimes, what seems right in theory doesn't work out in practice. Because of that, if your child starts staying home alone, watch for signs of stress. (See "Signs of Stress," at left.) If both you and your child prepare adequately for the new arrangement, but find it doesn't work, that's fine. Explain to your youngster that people often change their minds and that does not mean someone failed.

If possible, go back to the arrangement you were using before your child started staying home alone. Then, in six months or so, talk with your youngster again about staying at home alone.

Signs of Stress

Just like adults, youngsters often are under stress. This stress can show up in a number of ways. If you notice any of the following problems, you'll need to find out what's wrong in your child's life so you can begin to deal with it. Don't automatically assume that stress is to blame, however. Some signals could be indicative of physical rather than emotional problems.

● Does your youngster complain of stomachaches, headaches, or vague and undefined illnesses?

● Does your child have difficulty sleeping or complain of being tired all the time?

● Does your child have reoccurring nightmares?

● If your youngster has allergies or is asthmatic, have you noticed an increase in attacks?

● Has your child become more irritable, careless, or unenthusiastic?

● Does your youngster have difficulty concentrating? Does he jump from one activity to another? Does he seem nervous much of the time?

● Has there been a sudden or dramatic increase or decrease in your youngster's effort on schoolwork?

● Is your youngster falling behind classmates in academic work?

● Has school attendance become erratic?

● Does your child jokingly talk about committing suicide?

NUTS AND BOLTS

The more you and your youngster have prepared for the latchkey arrangement ahead of time, the more successful it will be. The best way to prepare is by anticipating different situations before they occur, then discussing how they should be handled. That way, a lot of problems can be avoided altogether.

By playing "what if" games, you'll help your youngster analyze problems and develop good judgment. Ask your youngster what he'd do if there were a bad storm, or if you wanted him to run the dishwasher, or if a stranger repeatedly called him on the telephone. When you clearly outline what the child needs to do without you around, you'll encourage responsibility. And by knowing what to expect from day to day, your child will feel confident about handling situations. This added dose of security certainly can't hurt!

Tour the House

One of the first things to do to prepare your youngster for staying alone is to tour the house with your child. Have the child bring along a pad of paper and a pencil to write down instructions. Here's what you should look for:
- Are there any pieces of equipment that you do not want your youngster to operate when you're gone? The stereo system? The compact disc player? Depending on your youngster's age and experience, you may not want her to use the kitchen stove or the food processor. Ask your child to make a list of hands-off items.
- Are there any games or toys that will be off-limits when your youngster has friends over and no adult is home?
- List the equipment that your youngster should know how to use in your absence.

How about the telephone answering machine or a videocassette recorder? If you'll want your child to put a load of clothes in the washing machine, or run the dishwasher, don't assume the youngster understands all the buttons and knobs. Have your child make a list of the equipment he'll need to learn to operate. Then, set aside a sufficient amount of time for learning.
- If you want the first-floor curtains closed while you're gone, explain that it's so strangers can't see that your child is the only one home. Then, ask your youngster to make sure they're closed when she gets home from school.
- If the house feels too hot or too cold, will you allow your child to adjust the thermostat? If so, explain how it works.
- Discuss the possibility of bad storms, and show your youngster where to go for safety.
- Similarly, discuss the possibility of a fire. Your family already should have two plans of escape that you should practice often with your youngster.

Vital Information

There aren't special secrets to latchkey success, but there are at least three necessary components: a house key that works, access to a parent, and a helpful neighbor.

Keeping track of the key. Carrying and using a house key will be one of the biggest responsibilities your youngster must assume. But there are plenty of hints for helping the child prepare for that responsibility:
- Make sure names and an address *do not* appear on your child's key or the key chain. Explain to your youngster that labeling the key makes it too easy for a person who finds a lost key to break into the house.

NUTS AND BOLTS

● Some keys work any way they're placed in the keyhole; others work only a certain way. If yours works only a certain way, mark the "top" of the key with fingernail polish. Likewise, if your door has more than one lock and key, mark the key and corresponding lock with fingernail polish.

● Let your youngster practice using the key until he feels confident that he can do it when he's alone.

● Tell your youngster that if she ever has trouble getting the key to turn, she should go to a neighbor's house for help. Explain that pressing too hard can bend or break the key.

● If you have a combination entry lock on your door, help your child memorize the series of buttons that must be pushed to gain entry.

● Have the youngster carry the house key on a string or chain around his neck. Or, attach the string to a belt loop and put the key in a pants pocket. Remind the child to keep the key hidden during the day.

● Explain to your youngster that she shouldn't tell anyone about the key—even a friend. Also, forbid the child to loan the key to anyone.

● Keep a spare key with a neighbor, *not* in the milk box or mailbox, or under the doormat. These are the very places a burglar is most likely to look.

● Make sure your youngster always carries enough change for a telephone call. Or, keep extra coins hidden outside your home. That way, if the key gets lost and the neighbors aren't home, your child can call you from a pay telephone. While that may be inconvenient, it's better than having a frightened youngster waiting outside the house for you, especially in the winter when it's cold and darkness comes early.

Calling you at work. When your youngster begins staying home alone, the telephone becomes a lifeline between the two of you. Explain to your youngster that he'll be expected to check in with a phone call every day after school. Tell him that skipping the call makes parents worry.

Telephone Numbers Your Child Will Need

Chances are, your youngster already has memorized your work numbers, plus the numbers of several friends. But for the child who's staying home alone, knowing emergency numbers and the numbers of special neighbors and relatives also becomes important.

Help your youngster put the names and telephone numbers he'll need to know in the special "telephone directory" at the back of this book. Remind your youngster that the directory is his very own, and can be used to list nonemergency as well as emergency numbers. As your child fills in the blanks, discuss why certain numbers are important:

● Special neighbors will help if a problem can't wait until Mom or Dad gets home. Ideally, provide your child with the numbers of two neighbors, in case one isn't home.

● Kids know they can call Grandma or Grandpa about *anything*. However, if that means long-distance charges, you may need to establish some rules.

● Discuss when to use the different emergency numbers: 911, 0, or numbers for the doctor, ambulance, poison control center, and police and fire departments. Generally speaking, in an emergency, your child should dial 911 or 0 for the quickest results.

● Find out if your community has a hot line for latchkey kids. Adult volunteers answer the hot lines and talk with children about their days, answer questions about homework, or help calm fears.

Likewise, explain to your youngster that she cannot call you at work whenever the desire strikes. Discuss "what if" situations to help her understand when to call and when not to call.

Set up some guidelines for using the telephone:

- If you're able to receive phone calls at work, be available for that all-important after-school call. If possible, take a few minutes to chat about the day's events. The news that kids want to share at 3 o'clock may be long forgotten by suppertime.
- If neither you nor your spouse can easily receive calls during work hours, make arrangements for one of you to call your child every day at a certain time.
- If neither of you is able to make a call, have your youngster call another designated adult each day after school.
- If your youngster goes to a friend's house after school, make sure you have a number where the child can be reached.

Making arrangements with neighbors. It's certainly ideal to have several trustworthy neighbors who are home during the day and who are willing to help your child when necessary. Explain to the neighbors that your child will be taking care of himself, then ask if the child may contact them in case of an emergency.

- Don't assume that because you know the neighbors well, your child does, too. Visit the neighbors several times with your youngster. It's important that the child feels comfortable around them.
- Leave an extra key with these neighbors.
- You can't expect your neighbors to notify you every time they go away. But you can ask them to let you know if they'll be gone for a long period of time. In such instances, you will want to make backup arrangements.
- Share your house rules with your neighbors. That way, if you've decided only one playmate is allowed at your house after

school and the neighbors see your yard full of kids, they'll have a sense of whether Mom or Dad should be called.

- From time to time, drop off a little present for the neighbors, just to let them know their assistance is appreciated.

Etcetera, Etcetera

Transportation. Getting your latchkey child to and from school and other activities can present real problems. What if your child misses the school bus? What if she's still in pajamas when the car pool arrives? What if she must walk five blocks home in the pouring rain?

Planning ahead, insisting that your youngster accept responsibility, and enforcing the rules with prearranged consequences are your best bets for dealing with the problems that might occur. Some suggestions are:

- Set the exact time your child must be ready to leave for school. Make it five minutes earlier than necessary.
- Discuss how important it is that your child be ready on time. (Missing a ride might mean taking a cab or that a parent must leave work to take the child to school.) Help your youngster understand that his actions also affect other people.
- Determine beforehand the consequences for not being ready on time. Then, if your youngster misses a ride due to her own negligence, enforce those consequences.
- If your child walks to school, arrange an alternative for inclement weather. Your child may need to take a cab or ride with a friend or relative who's willing to drive the youngster. Or, you may need to arrange with your work supervisor for you to arrive late or leave early occasionally.

Feeling Sick?

Perhaps nothing is more agonizing to a working parent than having a sick child. Whether the youngster gets sick before you leave for work or becomes ill at school, the guilt most parents face if they aren't able to be with their child is enormous.

Obviously, if your child becomes gravely ill, you may need to make arrangements to stay home so you can care for the child.

Also, plan ahead for those days when your youngster might get sick at school and you aren't able to bring the child home. Make prior arrangements with a neighbor or relative so you can call them to pick up the child.

Most of the time, "sick" is the 24-hour flu, a sore throat, or the sniffles, which aren't fun but certainly aren't devastating. In such mild situations and if your child is already staying home alone for some part of the day, she should be able to care for herself. Still, there are things you can do to help both you and your youngster:

● Make a comfortable spot on the living-room or family-room sofa, complete with a blanket and extra pillows. Set a box of tissues and a big glass of juice near the sofa before leaving for work.

● Find a couple of good books for your youngster to read, and leave a deck of cards or other activities next to the sofa. If your child is sick for several days, bring home some library books. If you need suggestions, see the librarian.

● Come home at noon and fix lunch for yourself and your youngster. If that's not possible, ask a neighbor to drop in once during the day. Be sure your child knows when the neighbor will check in, so the youngster isn't startled. And make sure the neighbor has a key.

● Call several times during the day. But avoid calling during the middle of the afternoon since that's when sick kids—just like sick adults—like to nap.

● If your youngster is on medication, measure the proper doses, along with easy-to-understand instructions, before leaving for work. Explain the importance of not taking more than the doctor prescribed.

● Finally, check with your school about the possibility of dropping your child off early or picking the youngster up late. Some schools provide care for students before and after school. However, if your school does not have that service, the staff may not be pleased with you if your child remains after school hours.

Eating breakfast. For working parents, mornings can be a real zoo. Mom and Dad may simplify the routine by cutting out their own breakfasts, but that's a poor example to set for a child. Or, parents in a hurry may fix the morning meal without much regard for nutrition.

Your youngster cannot afford to miss a good breakfast. With some forethought, a nutritious breakfast can become part of the early-morning routine:

● Plan a week's worth of morning meals each time you make out your grocery-shopping list.

● Stock up on fresh fruits. They're easy to prepare and good for everyone.

● When your youngster gets old enough to fix her own breakfast, help plan balanced menus that your child can prepare easily.

● If you're consistently rushed in the morning, get up 15 minutes earlier. Good breakfasts, such as whole-grain cereals and toast, don't take a long time to fix.

● If you must leave the house before your youngster is awake, make arrangements to get your child up with sufficient time to fix

and eat a good breakfast. (Having your youngster set an alarm clock will do more to encourage responsibility than calling the youngster once you get to work.)
• Your youngster will be more likely to prepare his own breakfast if the table already is set and the meal is started. For instance, place the cereal in a bowl and leave cut-up fruit in the refrigerator.

School lunch. With a little planning, school lunch will be no problem:
• Purchase several hot-lunch tickets at one time. Have your youngster write her name on the back of each ticket and keep them in her room. Remembering to take one to school every day teaches responsibility.
• If your school provides a card that is punched, make the youngster responsible for his own card.
• If your child carries her lunch, plan several cold-lunch menus with her. Keep as many of the items on hand as possible.
• Decide one week in advance which days your youngster will eat hot lunch and which days he will take a sack lunch. Either make the lunch or have your youngster stick a lunch ticket in his schoolbag the night before.
• Ask the school what happens if your child appears without a card, ticket, or a lunch from home. Most likely, the teacher will "lend" a hot-lunch ticket. Help your youngster understand that it is her responsibility to pay the teacher back.

After-school activities. There seems to be ample opportunity for youngsters to participate in organized after-school activities and lessons—from soccer to softball, dancing to art classes. And for the latchkey kid, one or two such activities may be a welcome relief from the daily boredom of being in an empty house. On the other hand, scheduling an activity for every afternoon isn't fair, either. Kids need some quiet, unstructured time to themselves, too.

Again, careful planning is the key to success:
• Allow your youngster to help select one or two activities.
• First, consider any opportunities that are available in the school building or on school grounds. Many organizations such as Scouts and Camp Fire have meetings in the school, partly because that eliminates transportation problems.
• Explain to your youngster that providing transportation from school to an activity at another location, and from the activity home, will be a factor in whether or not he can sign up.
• See if you can carpool with other parents. If another parent can drive right after school, you may be able to pick the kids up afterward.
• If carpooling can't be arranged, hire a teenager or older adult in your neighborhood to drive.
• Or, consider using public transportation.
• Depending on the distance and amount of traffic, your youngster may be able to walk or ride a bike.
• If possible, arrange for your child to go to the public library after school one afternoon each week. The youngster can read or do homework, and you can pick her up on your way home from work. Make sure, however, that your youngster wants to go to the library and understands the importance of abiding by the rules. After all, you don't want to use the library as a temporary baby-sitting service.

Anticipating glitches. No matter how well you plan for your child's time before and after school, glitches will pop up. That's when patience and good listening skills come into play.

Discuss each problem that arises with your youngster, and ask the child for suggestions on how the situation could have been handled differently. The positive approach—looking for better solutions—makes more sense than the negative approach—complaining when something goes wrong.

Encouraging your youngster to find better solutions also puts some of the responsibility on your child the next time a similar situation occurs. And nurturing that sense of responsibility is one of the biggest opportunities in the latchkey arrangement.

LETTING YOUR CHILD STAY HOME ALONE

Youngsters don't suddenly walk or talk in complete sentences. They don't suddenly know how to dribble a basketball or ride a bicycle. Likewise, they aren't suddenly equipped to stay home alone. Staying alone is like any other skill. It requires independence and responsibility, qualities you can help a child develop. As with everything else, it just takes time and practice.

An Hour at a Time

Begin preparing your child for the latchkey arrangement by leaving the youngster alone at first for only short periods of time. Exactly when you can start this practice depends more on your child's maturity than on the youngster's chronological age.

Talk with other parents who have youngsters your child's age. If another parent occasionally leaves his child home alone for a little while, ask how the child is adapting to the experience.

Likewise, listen to your youngster. If she has friends who stay home alone for short periods of time, you'll hear about it. (Kids are great imitators; they want to do what others are doing.) If the idea of being in charge—even for an hour or so—appeals to your youngster *as well as* to you, it's time to give independence a try. Here are some tips:

- Discuss where you'll be when your youngster is home alone. Ideally, the first time, choose a place familiar to your youngster, such as a friend's house. That way, your child can picture where you will be.
- The first few times, go places where you can be reached easily by telephone. Don't encourage your child to call you, but reassure him that a phone call is possible, if necessary.
- Make sure your child understands how long you'll be gone. Tell her what time you'll return, set a timer for the amount of time you'll be away, or tell her you'll return before the TV show she's watching is over.
- If, after you've left, you discover you'll be late getting home, call your child. Five or 10 minutes may not seem like much to you, but it can be an eternity to a youngster who's just getting accustomed to staying at home alone.
- When you get home, spend a few minutes with your youngster. Ask what happened while you were gone. Keep your questions positive. Don't ask, "Were you afraid while I was away?" Instead ask, "How did it feel to be in charge?"
- There's a fine line between encouraging safe, responsible behavior and instilling fear in your youngster. Rather than dwelling on the bad things that can happen when your child is home alone, discuss the kind of behavior that will keep your youngster safe and sound.

Staying Home Alone During the School Year

Home alone after school. While there's no rule that says a latchkey kid should begin staying home alone after school rather than before school, that's the route most parents choose for several reasons.

No meals are necessary after school, whereas in the morning a child may need to fix all or part of breakfast.

Similarly, when a child comes home from school, there's usually no rush to go somewhere. In the morning, kids have a time schedule to follow—whether it's catching the school bus or car pool, or joining other children who walk to school. And meeting those time guidelines can be as stressful to your child as meeting work deadlines is for you. A youngster who is left home alone in the morning before he can handle the responsibilities of fixing breakfast and getting out the door on time may not have a good initial latchkey experience.

The child who already has stayed home alone for an hour or so should adjust well to being in charge after school. The big difference is that, after school, your youngster enters an empty house. That's different from staying home while the parent leaves for a while. But there are ways you can help your youngster adjust:

- Talk with your youngster about coming home to an empty house. Otherwise, initially the quiet house may be overwhelming.
- Ask a librarian or your child's teacher for a good storybook about latchkey kids that your child can read. Once the youngster is finished with the book, ask her to share what she's learned with you. Discuss how the characters in the book handle staying at home alone.

- Let your youngster use his own house key when you go on family outings. The practice will help him feel confident that he can lock and unlock the door once he's alone.
- When your youngster first begins coming home alone after school, set aside time each evening to talk about her experience. Ask open-ended questions and listen carefully to the answers. Your purpose is to find out how she *feels* about coming home alone.
- If you detect any problems, deal with them right away. Don't assume the problems will go away by themselves.

Home alone before school. Many factors will enter into a decision to begin leaving your youngster alone before school:
- Will your child get up and eat breakfast without you there?
- Will your youngster leave for school on time?
- Does the child want to stay home alone before school? (That desire may be based partly on what classmates are doing.)

Once you and your youngster have decided that being alone before school is OK, there are some tips both of you can follow to make that rushed time flow smoothly.
- Go through a dry run on the weekend to see how long it takes your youngster to get ready for school and eat breakfast without any assistance from you. Then add an extra 10 minutes in case something goes wrong.
- With that time frame in mind, have your youngster begin setting her own alarm clock and getting herself up—if she isn't already doing so.
- Encourage your youngster to lay out school clothes the night before. Place the house key with the clothes.
- Reserve a spot close to the door where the youngster can put school materials—perhaps a project or a report, a book the child is reading, a lunch ticket, or a bus pass.

Home Alone After Dark

Staying home alone during the day and being the only one home after dark are two very different things. Even youngsters who demonstrate little hesitation about becoming a latchkey kid may be apprehensive when it comes to spending evenings by themselves.

Because there's something eerie about nighttime, it's best not to leave your child alone after dark until the youngster has had plenty of experience with independence. Once your child handles the responsibilities of being alone before and after school, he may look forward to taking care of himself in the evening.

There are some things you can do to help your youngster prepare for that unique after-dark situation:

• Encourage her to express feelings about staying home alone after dark. Don't look for negatives, but don't ignore them either. Ignoring anxieties or fears won't make them go away. If your youngster expresses negative feelings, discuss them. Sometimes, sharing fears is the best way to alleviate them.

• If your child has a certain place in the house—the basement, for example—that seems particularly scary at night, explore it together.

• If you had nighttime fears as a young-ster, share them with your child. Knowing that Mom or Dad experienced similar apprehensions is helpful to a youngster.

• Begin by leaving your youngster home after dark for only short periods of time, such as one-half hour. Make sure the child knows where you'll be.

• If you can't be reached by phone, leave the number of a friend or neighbor who will be available if your youngster feels the need to call someone.

• Close first-floor curtains, so passersby can't look in the windows and see the child alone.

• Be selective about the television shows your youngster may watch. Avoid adult programs, especially ones that are scary or violent.

• If your youngster is truly afraid of the dark, put up a light outside your house or apartment. Turn the light on nightly, not just when your youngster is home alone. That way, it does not signal to anyone that a child is the only one home.

• Until your youngster is accustomed to staying home alone in the evenings, try to be home before the child's bedtime. If you cannot, arrange for an older teenager or neighbor to come in at your child's bedtime and stay until you return.

• Post a calendar marked with after-school activities and remind your youngster to check it nightly. If there's an activity scheduled for the next afternoon that will require equipment (a Scout handbook, a soccer ball, or paints and brushes for an art class), have the child leave those materials by the door as well.

• If you know your youngster is a dawdler, insist that television stay off in the morning. It's too easy for a child to start watching a program and forget about the time.

• Post a list of duties that must be completed before your youngster leaves for school, such as turning off all lights and

LETTING YOUR CHILD STAY HOME ALONE

the radio, making sure windows are shut, and taking care of a pet.

● Remind your youngster how important it is to lock the door when leaving.

Staying Alone During School-Year Vacations

If your youngster's school calendar is like most, the kids have about two weeks off for winter holidays. Many school districts also provide a week-long spring break. Besides that, schools close for national holidays, inclement weather, parent-teacher conferences, and staff-development sessions.

But you aren't always home on those days. In fact, the majority of time kids are on break, parents are at work.

For latchkey kids just beginning to stay alone before and/or after school, spending an entire day—or week—home alone may be too much. If that's the situation at your house, have your youngster go back to the day-care center or baby-sitter you used before your child began staying alone. There are also day camps during winter holidays and spring breaks. Your youngster may enjoy the camp experience more than staying alone for days at a time. And the peace of mind you'll experience knowing your youngster is being cared for could be well worth the camp fee.

On the other hand, if your youngster has been taking care of herself before and after school long enough to feel confident about staying alone, these mini-breaks could be a good preparation for staying at home during summer vacation.

Talk it over. Discuss with your child the pros and cons of staying alone the entire day. Make sure both of you feel comfortable with the new arrangement.

Look upon the first vacation as a trial period. Remind your youngster that he first began staying alone before and after school on a trial basis, too. Help your youngster understand that if he spends the day alone and doesn't like it, other arrangements can be made. It's important that your youngster not feel trapped into something he is not ready for.

Establishing new rules. Staying alone all day calls for different rules than does spending a couple of hours alone before or after school.

For example, if you haven't allowed your youngster to have company after school, you might rethink that rule. Expecting a youngster to spend a whole week or even two at home with no one to play with seems unfair. Together, set up some rules that allow your child to have fun with a friend but still permit you to have peace of mind at work.

Some of your previously established rules now may need reconsideration. How much television may your youngster watch during the day? What are the rules for preparing breakfast and lunch? And how about cleaning up afterward? Since there may be no homework (and often no music or dance lessons as there are during the rest of the school year), how will your youngster spend the time generally used for studying or practicing? Some free time is wonderful, but too much free time can be a disaster.

Evaluating the results. If you and your youngster decide she can stay home alone during a school break, determine how you will measure the success of the trial run. Set goals, such as a clean kitchen every evening, completed chores, and a phone line that isn't busy from morning until night. Then each day, discuss how well each of those goals is being met. If you or your child find some goals are unrealistic, don't be afraid to revise them.

When goals are reached, praise your child. When the youngster falls short of goals, discuss what went wrong. See what can be altered to help your child achieve success the next day.

At the end of the school vacation, reward your youngster for a job well done. Take him out to lunch, shopping, or to a movie. That's a nice way to thank him for being responsible.

Staying Alone During The Summer Months

Once your youngster has stayed alone responsibly during school-year vacations, consider leaving her alone during summer vacation. But you'll find there's more involved than simply defining a few rules.

Summer vacation is a *long* time—too long to expect a youngster to spend five days per week at home alone with little or no structure. Even most adults get restless after a couple weeks of vacation. While adults may not always want to go back to work, most will admit that doing nothing gets boring.

Kids are no different. After lying under a tree or watching TV game shows for several weeks, kids are ready for something different. If you don't have activities and chores planned, you could be inviting trouble.

There are plenty of options to consider when making summer plans, but discuss them with your child several months before summer arrives. Some activities, such as summer camp and music lesson slots, fill up quickly. But, as you discuss options, remember that overscheduling your youngster's summer may be as bad as planning nothing at all. Kids need time to do nothing.

The programs you select should interest your youngster, be ones you can afford, and be spread throughout the summer.

Here are a few summer suggestions:

Day camps. In some areas, a bus picks up youngsters at a specific point each morning, then drops them off in the evening. Some specialized day camps zero in on one activity—swimming, tennis, music, soccer, or writing. Others offer a variety of activities from learning to cook over an open fire to hiking in the wilderness. Day camps are a good way for youngsters to have a camping experience.

Overnight camps. These camps can run from one week to all summer. As with day camps, these camping experiences may be specialized or very general. Usually, the more specialized a camp, the more expensive it will be. Often, however, financial assistance is available for qualifying students.

Vacation Bible schools. Many churches and synagogues offer one- to two-week sessions, and sometimes longer, for members' youngsters. Generally, classes are divided by age level, and combine learning about religion with crafts and recreation.

Parks programs. City parks and recreation departments sponsor full-day or half-day programs that include arts and crafts, field trips, and swimming. Generally, you can sign up for programs one week at a time.

Classes. If transportation is available, your youngster might take a class at the local art center or playhouse, or participate in swimming or soccer lessons. Lots of summer experiences such as these last only one or two hours each day, but give some structure to your child's week.

Visiting relatives. Grandparents, cousins, or an aunt and uncle are fun to visit and can provide your youngster with wonderful memories to last a lifetime. If you send your child to a relative's house, be sure your youngster and your relatives understand your expectations for good behavior.

Visiting friends. If your child has a good friend in another town, send your youngster to see him for a few days. If the friend pays a return visit to your house, be sure the parents understand that no adult is at home during the day. Enroll both children in an area day camp, so they have activities during the visit.

THE RULES OF THE HOUSE

Establishing the Rules

Rules provide structure for your youngster, help the child feel secure, and reflect your expectations of the child's behavior. The latchkey life flows much more smoothly for everyone when specific rules are in place and each family member knows what's expected of him or her.

Making rules together. How the rules are established can make a big difference in how well the rules are followed. You could draw up a list of dos and don'ts, hand them to your youngster, and announce that these are the rules she's expected to follow. But you'll probably get better results if you and your child take the opportunity to develop a set of guidelines together.

This chapter offers suggested rules for using the telephone, cooking, playing outdoors, and other situations that need consideration. Take time to adequately discuss the rules in every section, encouraging your youngster to express how he feels about them.

Talk especially about rules that may cause controversy, such as limiting phone conversations with friends or regulating the amount of television the child may watch. Ideally, the two of you will reach an agreement on such issues. But since that isn't always possible, you, with your judgment and maturity, probably will determine the ultimate decision.

After you and your youngster have discussed the rules suggested in this chapter, discuss any other rules that either of you thinks should be added to the list. Then, determine the consequences, so both of you—and particularly the child—know what will happen if a rule is broken.

Are the rules clear? Rules should be stated as clearly and specifically as possible. Instead of saying, "Take care of the breakfast dishes," say, "Wash the breakfast dishes, wipe off the table and counter, and put away the toaster before you leave for school."

Also, make sure you and your youngster have similar interpretations of the rules. The rule, "Never open the door to a stranger," may be so clear that no discussion is needed. But "Eat only a light snack after school," can be interpreted differently. Generally, what you call "light," a healthy, 12-year-old boy calls "meager."

Verbalize your interpretation of rules that fall into the gray area and ask your child to do the same. Where there's a difference, the two of you need to find a common ground for the rule's meaning.

You'll also find that a positive approach is more productive. "Please have the dinner table set by 5 p.m." sounds much more pleasant than "Don't turn on the television or call any friends until the table is set."

Finally, realize that you also have rules to follow. For example, if your youngster must call you every afternoon when she gets home from school, you must stay by the telephone to receive her call. If on a given day the child won't be coming home right after school or you'll be in a meeting at that time, other arrangements for checking in must be made ahead of time.

Posting the rules. Don't trust your memory or your youngster's. Instead, post the rules in a handy reference place, such as on the refrigerator door, a family room

THE RULES OF THE HOUSE

When Rules Are Broken

If you don't enforce house rules, you send your youngster a message that the rules weren't important in the first place. So, when rules are broken, you need to react. Here are some helpful guidelines:

● Your child just may have made a mistake, which isn't necessarily the same as breaking a rule. When it appears that a rule has been broken, begin by discussing the situation with your youngster to determine which was the case.

● If a mistake was made, help your youngster understand why her actions have caused a problem. Then assume the mistake will not reoccur.

● On the other hand, if the rule was deliberately broken, impose a consequence.

● Make the punishment consistent with the offense. It's probably worse to have five friends over after school (when the limit is one) than to talk for 20 minutes on the telephone (when the limit is 15 minutes).

● Make the punishment realistic. Insisting a youngster stay in his room after school makes little sense when no one's home to enforce the rule. Instead, deny a privilege, such as going to a friend's house to play.

● Enforcement of the rule should begin as quickly after you get home as possible. When you punish a youngster a week after the rule was broken, the consequence loses much of its effectiveness.

Reviewing the rules. Any time a dispute can't be settled by referring to the rules, discuss the rule in question. Even though your early efforts were aimed at avoiding misunderstandings, there's no guarantee that a misunderstanding won't occur.

Likewise, some of your rules may work better on paper than in practice. When a rule seems to be a constant source of irritation for either you or your youngster, it deserves a second look. There may be a better way of handling a situation.

Finally, as your child grows up, the rules need to change. A youngster beginning to stay home alone may not be physically ready—let alone mature enough—to use an oven. But a child who's been on his own for several years may be able and willing to start supper before you get home. To accommodate changes in your growing child, you should:

● Set aside time once or twice each year to review the rules with your child.

● Before the meeting, ask your youngster to make a list of the rules she would like to consider changing. Then, do the same yourself. Each of you should be prepared to say why a particular rule no longer works.

● When you reach an agreement on changes, make sure you both have the same interpretation of the new rule.

● Realize that your youngster can assume more responsibility every year and be willing to loosen restrictions accordingly.

● If you feel your child is asking for too much freedom too soon, you may want to ask your child's teacher how well the youngster accepts new responsibilities in school. Also, ask other parents what responsibilities their youngsters have assumed at home.

Enforcing the rules. Rules are intended to give you control over what's going on at home and to ensure that your child is safe when no adult is home. If you lose control, you may be placing your child in danger.

That's why it's very important that you stick by the rules you and your child have agreed upon. (See "When Rules Are Broken," at left.)

bulletin board, or the back of your youngster's bedroom door. It's important that your child can refer to the rules quickly when a question arises. It's equally important that you refer to them when a dispute arises.

Getting Specific

The telephone. When your child is home alone, the telephone becomes her primary connection with the outside world. Even so, unlimited telephone conversations aren't a good idea. These suggestions will help your youngster make good use of the telephone:
● Have your youngster call you or another adult every day when he gets home from school. It will give both of you a feeling of security.
● Set a time limit—15 minutes, perhaps—for your youngster's conversations with friends. Explain that it's important for you to be able to reach her on the phone in case of an emergency.
● Require at least a 15-minute interval between calls, so others trying to call your home can get through.
● Instruct your child to be polite to all callers. That means no screaming or yelling into the receiver.
● Tell your youngster to greet every caller with "Hello" rather than with a name.
● Under no circumstances should your child tell a caller that she's home alone. Instead, she should say that her parents can't come to the phone, but someone will return the call soon.
● Keep a pad and pencil by the phone. Instruct the child to ask if he can take a message. If the caller wants to leave a message, your youngster should write down the caller's name and number, and a brief message. (Set a good example by also taking messages for your youngster.)
● If the message is important and the child thinks it can't wait until you get home, have your youngster call you at work. Your child *should not* give out your work number.
● Tell your child not to talk to a prank caller. Instead, he should hang up and talk about it with you that evening.
● If she receives a lot of scary calls or if the same stranger calls repeatedly, instruct your child to call either you or another designated adult. You may want your youngster to go to a neighbor's house until you get home.

There are two telephone features that benefit the latchkey kid. "Call waiting" signals the person using the telephone that someone else is trying to call your home. If you have a youngster who is tethered to the phone, the feature eliminates the frustration for the caller of repeatedly listening to a busy signal.

Likewise, some answering machines allow you to listen to incoming calls. If the caller is a stranger, the child can simply allow the message to be recorded. If the child knows the caller, the youngster can switch off the machine and talk.

The television. Too much of one thing—including television—isn't healthy. Here are some guidelines to help you direct your child's viewing habits:
● Decide with your child how much TV she may watch each day. Explain that while watching television is one way to relax after school, tuning in for a long time can keep her from doing chores, homework, or other activities—even fun ones.
● To limit viewing time, select certain programs he may watch or set a time limit for watching.
● Help your youngster select an educational show to watch after school. Then, ask for a report on the program at supper. Ask whether or not it was a good show and why. Making such judgments will help the child become a more discerning viewer.
● If your youngster uses TV as a companion, suggest she do something else while watching a program, such as folding the laundry, drawing or coloring, doing needlework, or exercising.
● If you have several children at home alone, decide the night before what programs will be watched. If there's a disagreement, you can help settle it then.
● If your youngster is still watching television when you get home, ask the child to turn it off and talk about the day. Chances are, your youngster would rather talk to you than watch TV. Suggest that the two of you make dinner together and you can chat while you work.

THE RULES
OF THE HOUSE

● In general, most daytime shows are suitable for children. However, sometimes cable TV channels air shows during the day that you may not want your youngster to watch. Because of that, consider purchasing a cable channel lockout box that can be used with pay channels. There also are remote control units that have parental codes. Then, it will be impossible for the child to watch the shows you don't want her to see.

● Watching television isn't the only after-school activity available to your child. Suggest starting homework, reading a good book, keeping a diary, or starting or working on a collection.

The kitchen. All kids love to eat and lots of them also love to cook. In fact, by allowing your youngster to prepare snacks or begin the evening meal, you'll actually do the child a favor. Young adults who only know how to boil water can end up hungry when they begin living on their own.

Obviously, younger children will have more kitchen restrictions than older youngsters. But some basic safety rules apply to all children:

● Unless you or another adult is around, your youngster shouldn't use sharp knives. Instead, teach her to cut with a table knife.

● Some appliances, such as food processors with complicated instructions and sharp blades, should be off-limits for all youngsters. Put a "Do not use" sticker on any appliance that is not for children's use.

● Other appliances, such as an electric mixer, can be handled by older children who learn the dos and don'ts under your guidance. That includes a reminder to unplug the electric mixer when putting in or taking out the beaters.

● Explain the importance of keeping wet hands away from appliances as well as electrical outlets.

● If feasible, have your child use the microwave oven instead of either the stove or oven.

● If you don't have a microwave oven, remember that hot ovens and range tops can be dangerous. Young children should not prepare food that requires cooking or baking. Older youngsters should cook or bake with you around before using the stove or oven on their own.

● Explain the potential danger of getting fingers caught in the garbage disposal. Younger children should not operate one alone. Remind older youngsters to *always* turn off the disposal before putting hands near it.

Cooking limitations. How much you allow or ask your youngster to do in the kitchen depends upon the child's age and level of responsibility. Before letting your child cook alone, have the youngster practice the necessary skills while you're around.

Also, consider purchasing a cookbook geared to your youngster's age. Such books are filled with recipes that your child will find not only manageable but also enjoyable to prepare.

As your youngster experiences success in the kitchen, the child will be anxious to do more and more, so periodically revise the limitations the two of you have set.

Snacking. After school, most youngsters think they can't make it until supper without a snack. And that's OK if the snack is nutritious and doesn't ruin the child's appetite for supper.

Plan after-school snacks with your youngster and vary the offerings every couple of weeks. If your latchkey kid is young, purchase items that don't require preparation, such as granola bars, fresh fruit, or yogurt. An older youngster can prepare a plate of cheese and crackers, toast bagels or English muffins and spread them with peanut butter or jam, or heat frozen prepared snacks in the microwave. Children's cookbooks have entire chapters on easy-to-fix snacks that are fun to make and to eat.

Starting supper. As your latchkey kid improves his kitchen skills, consider asking him to do advance preparation for the evening meal. Not only will assisting with meals help you, but assuming new responsibilities is one of the benefits derived from the latchkey arrangement.

Choose after-school snacks that are easy for a young-ster to prepare alone and that won't spoil the child's appetite by suppertime.

THE RULES
OF THE HOUSE

Ask yourself:
● Is my youngster interested in helping with meal preparation?
● Does the child understand the techniques required?
● Has the child demonstrated the ability to do the required steps?
● Can the youngster understand the recipe?

At first, give your youngster easy tasks, such as making a tossed salad or baking a cake from a cake mix. As the child gets older, let her share in the menu planning. Pick out parts of the meal that she can prepare alone.

No matter what the task, write down the youngster's responsibilities the night before, including time guidelines. If your child will be using a recipe, read it over with him. That way, you can clear up any misunderstandings he may have. (And you can make sure you have all the ingredients.)

Cleaning up. Teach your child that cleanup is part of cooking. That includes:
● Rinsing dishes and putting them in the dishwasher or washing them in the sink, if you don't have a dishwasher;
● wiping off the counter and range top;
● wiping out the inside of the microwave oven, if spills occurred;
● putting ingredients and leftovers away.

Having friends over. One of the most difficult aspects of the latchkey arrangement is not being allowed to play with friends after school. Lots of parents do not allow other children in their homes when an adult is not present. Few thoughts put a working parent on edge more than the vision of a child at home with three friends.

Allowing your youngster to have company only when you're home may be an insufficient solution. By developing guidelines, you may set the stage for company after school. What you allow depends upon the children's ages and maturity, as well as whether the friends can walk to your home or have other safe transportation. Here are some guidelines:
● In most cases, you should limit your child to having one guest at a time. Other youngsters who want to tag along should be

Warding Off Loneliness

Child guidance counselors say one of the biggest problems latchkey kids encounter is loneliness. For the child who's accustomed to a day-care center or baby-sitter's home, the switch to an empty house can be difficult. The problem is compounded when parents are reluctant to allow outside play or playmates to visit.

Here are some suggestions to help ward off lonely feelings:
● Consider getting a dog or cat. Pets make wonderful companions and help erase the feeling of loneliness.
● Suggest one-person activities, such as flying a kite, knitting, and writing short stories. Then, let the child's own interests guide him as he selects the activities he wants to try.
● Well-intentioned as you might be, don't try to plan every minute of your youngster's day. Children can be very resourceful when it comes to entertaining themselves.
● Encourage creativity and fill potentially lonely hours by keeping a basic stable of art supplies at home: typing paper; poster paints or watercolors; paintbrushes; chalk and crayons; pens and pencils; construction paper; old magazines; and paste or glue.
● Communicate affection and love often. When you get home from work, give your child a big hug and tell her you really missed her that day.
● Set aside time regularly to go somewhere with your youngster— maybe for a long walk in the park or out to supper. Use the opportunity for good conversation. Encourage your youngster to share feelings and do the same yourself.

told by your child that they can come another day.

- Make arrangements the night before a friend is to come over. Be sure the other child's parents know there is no adult at your house immediately after school. Also, find out what time the guest is to go home and whether you or the other child's parents are responsible for transportation.
- Some schools have a rule that no youngster may go home with another child unless the visiting child brings a note from his parents. Check your school's policy, or you may end up with two disappointed kids at the end of the school day.
- Unless your child and her friend can walk home, discuss transportation. If your child rides on the bus or in a car pool, can the friend do so also?
- If your child has after-school duties, such as caring for a pet, make sure the youngster understands that he's still responsible for the chores even if a friend is along.
- Determine specific toys, games, or activities that are off-limits when no adult is home. For instance, using a chemistry set or puttering in the kitchen requires adult supervision.
- Encourage your youngster to leave the television off when a friend is around. There's so much more to do when two kids are together.
- Decide beforehand what your child should do if activity gets out of hand. If the friend lives nearby, it may be best for that child to go home. If that isn't possible, suggest the children play a different game, or watch television for a while. If that doesn't work, have your child call a neighbor.

Playing outside. Latchkey kids often tend to become sedentary. First, the youngsters sit most of the day in school. Then, because many parents are afraid to let their children play outside for safety reasons, the youngsters come home and sit in front of the television until supper.

But kids aren't made for sitting around. So if arrangements can be made to ensure your child's safety—and consequently your peace of mind—it's much better if your youngster can get some healthy, outdoor exercise. Here are some suggestions:
- Establish boundaries, such as the yard, the block, or the school playground. Make sure you and your child have the same set of boundaries in mind, and that your youngster understands why these limits must be observed.
- If chores or homework must be done, decide whether those tasks must be completed before your youngster goes out to play. Then, enforce the decision.
- Insist that your child let you or another adult know if she's going to be outside.
- Have your child change into play clothes before going outside.
- Insist that the youngster lock the door and take the key along, even if he is playing in your yard.
- If neighbor kids will be playing in your yard, decide if they will be allowed to go inside to get a drink or use the bathroom.
- Discuss where your child should go for help if someone gets hurt.
- Set time limits on outside play. If the child isn't in your own yard, have her check in periodically with another adult.
- If your latchkey kid is older, leaving a note may be sufficient when the child goes out to play. Be sure the youngster writes down where he'll be, how he can be reached, and when he'll be home. Have a predetermined place for all notes so you'll spot them as soon as you arrive home.
- If there's a stranger hanging around, your youngster should go into the house immediately, lock the doors, and call an adult.

Riding a bicycle. Whether or not you allow your child to ride a bike when she's alone will depend on your youngster's biking experience, the amount of traffic on the streets, and, most likely, whether friends are riding their bikes. Discuss boundaries and safety precautions. Remind your youngster to use hand signals and never to ride double.

Swimming. If you have a swimming pool, NEVER allow your youngster to use it when you're gone, even if the child is a good swimmer.

THE RULES
OF THE HOUSE

Siblings. If you have more than one child at home, no one needs to tell you that the whole latchkey picture changes. On the positive side, the children won't necessarily experience the loneliness that one child feels coming into an empty house every day. Likewise, in an emergency, there's often strength in numbers. If someone gets hurt, one youngster can stay with the victim while another calls for help.

But there's also the potential for sibling squabbles. After all, that happens when you're around. And with no adult supervision, the fighting and arguing are more likely to increase than disappear.

More often than not, the struggle will be over who's in charge. But that's a problem you can deal with ahead of time.

Some families ask the oldest sibling to be responsible for younger brothers and sisters. That even may be a paid position. Other families allow each youngster to be responsible for himself or herself. Which route you select will depend upon the age differences between your children, their maturity levels, and their ability to get along with each other.

Putting the oldest in charge. If there is a difference of three years or more, you may want the oldest child to take charge. That youngster needs to understand that her role is to remind younger siblings of the rules, but not to push too hard or to punish. Rather, her job is to care for brothers and sisters until a parent gets home. Obviously, there's a fine line here and it may require a lot of discussion to clarify roles. After all, Mom and Dad are still the disciplinarians.

If the oldest child is in charge, make sure the youngster also has sufficient time to develop his own friendships and his own activities. By relying on him to raise siblings in your absence, it's easy to turn the child into an adult too soon. If younger siblings need someone to stay with them on a daily basis, have a baby-sitter come in periodically to free up the older sibling.

Putting everyone in charge. If there is only a couple years' difference between sibling ages, the youngsters can be responsible for

themselves. Reducing interaction among the children is the best way to reduce conflicts. The key is to make sure each youngster has an equal amount of freedom and responsibility. Each child should have a personal house key, the same number of chores, the same opportunities to have friends over, and similar chances to participate in after-school activities. No matter who's in charge, the whole family should determine the rules together ahead of time. For example:

● Assign duties to each child. Make it clear that if one youngster doesn't get his work done, you and he will deal with it after you get home.

● Decide the night before which television programs will be watched. Then, if there's a disagreement, you'll be around to help settle it. If someone deviates from the plan the next day, you should impose consequences that evening.

● Rotate the privilege of having friends over so there isn't more than one guest in your home at a time. Set up a schedule so each sibling may invite friends home.

● Rotate kitchen duties. Have older children take turns preparing after-school snacks for everyone. Insist that each child help clean up or rotate that duty weekly.

● Assign meal preparation chores. Older siblings can help with the food preparation. Younger ones can set the table.

● Pick a "neutral place" for each child. If there's a fight, the youngsters can go to their own spots to be alone for a while.

● If the kids can't settle a fight, tell them to wait until you get home to discuss it.

● When it looks as if someone may get hurt or something may be broken, it's time to call the neighbor or a parent.

● Discuss the fact that older siblings have more freedom than younger ones. Point out that they also have more responsibilities, which is all part of growing up. You cannot treat all children alike because different ages allow for different experiences.

Handling the fight from afar. Nothing is more frustrating than for your youngsters to call you at work, each with his or her own explanation of what the other sibling is doing wrong. But it happens.

Chances are, you can't settle the dispute over the phone. (And chances are, the dispute will be forgotten by the time you get home.) But you can calm things down.

Rather than trying to figure out who did what, instruct the youngsters to go to their "neutral places" for a certain amount of time. Also, set a time that evening when you will discuss the problem with the youngsters. During that discussion, come up with a joint agreement.

Finally, indicate over the phone that unless your directives are followed, there will be consequences. If your directives aren't followed, impose those consequences once you get home.

Avoid leaving work to settle a dispute unless there's potential danger. Once you run home, you've started a habit that may be difficult to break.

Tattling vs. informing. It's important for your children to understand the difference between tattling (which nobody likes) and informing. Explain to the children that if one youngster is supposed to be doing household chores, but is watching television instead, it's probably tattling to tell you about it. If a child is supposed to be doing household chores, but is experimenting with an off-limits chemistry set instead, calling you is informing. Whenever there is danger, you need to know.

Changing rules with changing ages. As your youngsters grow, your family needs to re-evaluate assigned duties. This is especially true when an older sibling has been in charge of younger ones. As younger children take on more chores around the house, as well as assume more responsibility in caring for themselves, less overall responsibility should be expected from the older sibling.

The chores. While your youngster will disagree, assigning household chores is probably beneficial to the child. Tasks not only require a child to structure after-school time, but also help a youngster assume an active role in making the house run smoothly. They also teach children tasks they'll need to know how to do later in life.

● Determine with your youngster the chores to be completed. Then, help the child choose chores that are geared to her ability.

● Some chores, such as mowing the lawn, can be dangerous and should be done only when an adult is home.

● Make a list of household chores that need completing every week. Have your youngster check off each one as it is finished. Then, the child will see progress.

● If your youngster continually grumbles about the assigned chores, consider changing his duties.

● If your youngster has a pet, she should be expected to take care of the animal as soon as she gets home from school. That's one chore that can't be negotiated and that must be completed every day.

● Don't expect so much work out of the child that there's no time for play or relaxation. Chores are important, but they aren't the only concern your child should have after school.

● As your youngster gets older, it becomes easy to add responsibilities to his chore list. But even older latchkey kids need time for themselves. Rather than making your youngster's list longer, change the chores to match his new level of maturity. For example, instead of having him set the table for supper, let him prepare the evening's salad or main dish.

Homework and practicing. Planning ahead so tasks are accomplished on time is tough for adults—it's often impossible for kids. If your youngster has a lot of home-work or if homework takes the child a long time, suggest that some of it be done before supper.

Likewise, if your youngster plays a musical instrument, suggest she practice part of the lesson before supper.

Making a schedule. To help your child get his tasks done and still have time for fun, make a schedule with him. For example:

3:30–4 p.m.: Play with the dog.
4–4:30 p.m.: Practice piano.
4:30–5 p.m.: Chores.

PLAYING IT SAFE AND SECURE

It's vital that your youngster feel safe and secure when home alone. You can help nurture those feelings by implementing safety measures around your house, helping your youngster develop personal safety skills, and establishing some safety rules before your child becomes a latchkey kid. As your youngster's feeling of security increases, the child's confidence that she can take care of herself will grow, too, and her fear of staying alone will decrease.

Checking Out the House

Begin by conducting a room-to-room safety check of your house with your youngster. As you go through the house, explain different situations your child may face when staying alone, and discuss how to handle them.

Listen carefully to your youngster's concerns about safety. Don't ignore his anxiety about being home alone. Instead, reassure him that even adults feel anxious when facing new situations. Suggest that listening to music, turning on lots of lights, or watching television for a while may help his anxiety to fade.

Here are some situations to check out on your safety tour:
● Show your child how to lock and unlock all the doors in the house, including the side door in an attached garage.
● Test your child's house key and the back-up key you will leave with a neighbor. If a key isn't precisely cut, it won't work.

● Is there a window near the front door or a peephole in the door, so your youngster can see who's outside without opening the door? If not, you may want to install one.
● Do all the windows on the ground floor lock? If not, have locks or safety devices installed.
● Are flashlights stored in handy places on each floor of the house, in case the electricity goes out? Check the batteries periodically.
● Explain that under no circumstances should your child light a candle instead of using a flashlight.
● Keep a battery-powered radio in the basement or wherever your family goes in case of a severe storm. If such a storm occurs when your child is home alone, the youngster at least will have a radio connecting her with the outside world.
● Make sure the batteries in your fire or smoke detectors work. Some smoke detectors emit a beep when the batteries need replacing. This unfamiliar noise could frighten or confuse your child, so acquaint your youngster with that sound.
● Likewise, set the detector off so your youngster will know what it sounds like.
● Check the condition of your appliance cords. Replace cords showing frayed wires and bare metal.
● Do you have too many cords plugged into a single outlet? Such an overload may cause a fire.
● Get rid of stacks of old newspapers, cans of old paint, and piles of oily rags (especially

those near heat sources). All of these items are fire hazards.

● Explain that matches, cans of gasoline or barbecue lighter fluid, lawn and garden chemicals, household cleaners, medicines, knives, and sharp tools are off-limits.

● Don't ask your youngster to operate the lawn mower or a snowblower when the child is home alone.

● Tell your youngster that if she smells gas, she is to leave the house immediately. Instruct her to go to a neighbor's house and have an adult call either the gas company or the fire department.

● Explain that if the toilet is running, he should jiggle the handle a few times. In most instances, that's all that is needed.

● Broken pipes and plugged toilets can make a big mess, so locate the shut-off valve for each sink and toilet in the house. Instruct your child how to shut those valves and the main water valve into the house as well.

● Label each breaker. Then, when you feel your youngster is sufficiently mature, show him where the circuit breaker box is located. Teach him to reset the switch when the circuit is tripped.

Reviewing the Safety Rules

Chances are, your youngster has been learning safety rules since kindergarten or even preschool days. Still, it's important to review those rules.

Avoiding strangers. Obviously, not every stranger is bad. But to be safe, a child should avoid all strangers.

● If your youngster walks to and from school, arrange for her to walk with other children, if possible.

● Unless it's an emergency, you should never send an unfamiliar person to pick up the child at school.

● Decide on a "secret code" word. In emergencies, if you must send an unfamiliar

person to pick up your child, have that person use the code word. Then, your youngster will know it's safe to leave with that person.

● Tell your child to stay away from strangers' cars, even when the driver stops to talk. Instead, the youngster should keep on walking and tell the stranger to ask an adult for help.

● Instruct your youngster to yell loudly if someone grabs her.

● If someone is following your youngster home, your child should go immediately to a nearby neighbor's house, a store, office building, or Blue Star home or its equivalent and call you from there. That way, the stranger won't know where your child lives.

● When the child is at home and a stranger comes to the door, your youngster should not let the person in *for any reason.* That includes people who want to use the telephone or the bathroom, unexpected delivery or repair persons, or someone who says he or she is a friend of the family.

● If the stranger says there has been an accident and someone is hurt, your child still should not open the door. Instead, your youngster should call a neighbor, an emergency number, or the number requested by the stranger.

Entering the house. If your youngster comes home from school and sees a window open, the door ajar, or any other telltale sign of trouble, the child should not go inside. Instead, she should go to a neighbor's home and call the police.

Thunderstorms. Storms can be scary even when parents are home, but they're doubly frightening to a youngster home alone. Still, most storms aren't dangerous. Your youngster should go inside if he sees a thunderstorm coming. He risks getting hit by lightning if he stands outside in the open or underneath a tree. Also, your child can listen to the radio or television for more information on the storm.

In Case of Fire

Have a family-evacuation plan for fires. Reinforce the necessity of following that plan, even if a fire breaks out when no one else is home.

● Prepare a diagram of your house and determine escape routes from each room. Draw them in.

● Tell your youngster never to attempt to put out a fire, no matter how small it is.

● Emphasize that getting out of the house is of primary importance. No one should go back into the house for anything— even the family pet.

● Keep rope ladders on upper floors to use for escape. Make sure your child understands how they work, as well as how to open the window and perhaps how to remove or knock out the screen or storm window.

● If you live in an apartment building, discuss why your youngster must use the stairs instead of an elevator.

● Decide on a central location for each member of the family to go to immediately after leaving the house.

● When everyone is outside and accounted for, call the fire department from a neighbor's phone. Be sure to give the fire department a name and address before hanging up.

● If you have several children at home, be specific about which older siblings are in charge of the younger ones. Also, be specific about who is to call the fire department from the neighbor's house.

● As a family, practice the fire drills often, using various escape routes.

● Because during a fire rooms may be smoky, practice leaving the house by crawling on your hands and knees. Remember that breathing deeply may be dangerous. In the event of a real fire, it's best to cover your mouth with a wet cloth, if possible.

● Practice with your child what to do if clothes catch on fire. Stop, drop to the floor or the ground, and roll around until the fire is out.

● Teach your child that if he's behind a closed door, he should feel the door to see if it's hot instead of opening it. If the door is hot to the touch, he should seal the cracks with towels or clothing, then escape through a window.

Reacting to an emergency. No matter what the emergency, your youngster must remember to stay calm. That will be especially difficult with no adult around. However, knowing ahead of time what to do will increase your youngster's confidence in his ability to handle any situation.

Handling First Aid

It would be nice if injuries, accidents, and illnesses occurred only when you were home. But every parent knows that simply isn't the case.

So it's imperative that you teach your child basic first aid. Having those skills will give your youngster the confidence and ability to handle simple situations, such as a scraped knee, a nosebleed, or a small burn.

If there is a first-aid course offered for children in your community, enroll your youngster. If not, ask the librarian for books on first aid that are written at the child's level. Or check with your pediatrician for materials.

Also, go over the First-Aid Rules on page 63 with your child. Discuss the situations your child is most likely to encounter when staying alone. Explain the dos and don'ts— why you *do* wash off a scrape with soap and warm water, why you *don't* move an

PLAYING IT
SAFE AND SECURE

unconscious person. Understanding the "why" behind a procedure will help your youngster think more clearly in a tense situation.

Help your youngster practice procedures, such as taking a temperature, cleaning and applying an adhesive bandage to a small imaginary cut, and caring for a small imaginary burn. The better understanding your youngster has of basic first-aid principles, the better she will deal with accidents or injuries when they occur.

How much can a child handle? The kinds of first-aid situations your youngster can handle depend upon the child's age and maturity. Obviously, an older child can deal with more difficult situations than a younger child. But don't expect too much from a child, no matter what his age. After all, many adults function poorly when even a minimal amount of first aid is required.

Once your youngster feels comfortable with first-aid basics, ask lots of "what if" questions to help her learn to recognize the difference between a situation she can handle by herself and one requiring outside help. Together, determine the situations requiring adult help. Determine who the adult will be and talk about alternatives in case that adult is not available. In most cases, the adult will be the neighbor who has agreed to help out when the need arises. But if that neighbor isn't available, your youngster may need to seek adult assistance via the telephone.

Periodically review the guidelines as your child matures and can take on more responsibility.

First-aid kit. You already may have a first-aid kit in your home, but chances are it's outfitted for an adult user who is able to handle more difficult situations than a youngster. Consequently, it may contain more items than your youngster will need. Put together a first-aid kit designed specifically for the simple situations your youngster can handle.

Let your child help assemble the kit. As you do that, discuss how each item in the kit will be used. Then, have your youngster practice using each item before putting it in the kit.

Here's what should go into the kit:
● A cotton washcloth or hand towel for cleaning cuts;
● A box containing bandages of various sizes for small cuts and scrapes;
● Gauze pads and adhesive tape for covering large cuts;
● A small pair of scissors to cut the tape;
● An elastic bandage for use on a sprained ankle, wrist, knee, or hand;
● Calamine lotion for insect bites;
● A bottle of aspirin substitute for headaches;
● Tweezers for removing slivers;
● An antibiotic ointment for minor scrapes or cuts;
● Temperature strips that are placed on the skin. While they don't provide as accurate readings as a thermometer, there is no danger of glass breaking in the child's mouth.

Also, keep an ice pack in the freezer. Or, show your youngster where you keep plastic bags that can be filled with ice cubes to put on a sprain or bruise.

Knowing When to Take Pills/Medicine

Instruct your child not to take any medicine without your permission. Even the aspirin substitute and the ointment in the first-aid kit should not be used unless an adult is consulted first.

Such instructions may mean you'll receive a phone call at work if your youngster comes home with a headache or a sore throat, or if the child falls and scrapes a knee. But such a call may be warranted, since youngsters do not have the maturity to decide when they should use medication.

If your child is taking medicine ordered by the pediatrician, measure and mark the correct amount the night before. If your youngster is to take the medicine more than once a day, measure and number each dosage. Make sure your youngster understands why he is *never* to take more than the prescribed dosage. Kids, like some adults, often mistakenly believe that if some medicine is good, more will be better. Likewise, explain why it's dangerous to take medicine that's been prescribed for another member of your family. It's best to keep other family members' medication hidden and out of reach.

Taking medicine at school. Most schools do not allow a student to keep medication in a desk or locker, nor to be responsible for taking it. Instead, the school nurse dispenses any medication taken during school hours. Your school nurse may ask you to fill out a permission-to-dispense-medication slip that will go on file in the nurse's office.

If your child must take medicine at school, put the medicine and instructions with the youngster's other materials to go to school so she won't forget it when she leaves for school. Generally, the student must take the medicine to the nurse's office before the school day starts.

Knowing When to Call for Help

There's a fine line between when you should foster independence and when you should encourage youngsters to seek adult assistance for problems. Unfortunately, there aren't any hard-and-fast rules to help youngsters identify on which side of the line a situation falls.

Knowing when to call. If you believe your child calls you or another adult for help when the youngster probably could

handle a situation alone, talk about it. Maybe your child just needs a vote of confidence from you.

Conversely, if your youngster attempts to handle situations that you believe are too complex for a child to deal with alone, explain your reasons. Point out the potential dangers. Help your youngster understand that seeking adult help is sometimes the mature way to handle a situation.

Knowing who to call. Discuss hypothetical situations to help your youngster identify who to call in different instances. If there's a fire, for example, your youngster should notify the fire department before calling a parent. But if your youngster has a headache or a fever, he should contact you or another adult, not a doctor.

A neighbor to call on. The neighbor who has consented to be on-call in your absence obviously provides an ideal source of help in emergencies. If the neighbor is going to be out of town, make arrangements for a back-up neighbor.

911. Some communities have the 911 emergency phone system, which allows callers to call one number for any type of emergency. The system also will help contact parents.

Instruct your child that when she calls 911, she should give her name and address, and describe the emergency. Then, she should remain on the line to give more information or to receive instructions about what to do.

If your area does not have 911, your youngster can dial "0" for operator if he can't readily find the numbers for the fire department, police, or ambulance. Many phones now are programmable, making it easy to call emergency numbers by punching a particular number or symbol. If you have a programmable phone, show your youngster how to use it. Also, make sure your child has quick access to the phone number for the doctor. Tell your child which hospital your family prefers to use.

USING YOUR COMMUNITY RESOURCES

You are not the only person concerned about the welfare of your child. A number of community resources are designed to make the latchkey arrangement as positive as possible for both you and your youngster.

Making Use of Latchkey Hot Lines

Some communities have telephone hot-line numbers for latchkey kids. Volunteers staff the phones for a few hours after school. Youngsters are encouraged to call, whether they're seeking information or reassurance. One caller may want to know at what temperature to set the oven to heat a casserole for supper. The next caller may be lonely and not able to reach Mom or Dad. Usually, callers just want to talk to an adult for a few minutes.

Often latchkey kids call because they are afraid—they've seen a stranger in the neighborhood, the child has received a prank phone call, or there's a loud thunderstorm. The volunteer may give the youngster specific instructions, such as telling her to lock the front door, or offer suggestions in case the youngster receives a second prank call. Or, the adult may simply chat with the child for a while, to calm the youngster's fears.

Finding an organization in your community with a hot-line number may be difficult since there's generally no clearinghouse for information about latchkey children. Often, a social service agency dealing with children's issues will know of a local hot line. Or the school counselor may have the phone number.

If your community has a hot-line number, post it in a prominent place or include it with the list for phone numbers at the back of this book. Encourage your youngster to use the number if she can't reach a parent or another adult.

Latchkey Learning In the Schools

Gone are the days when schools dealt strictly with reading, writing, and arithmetic. Today, programs to help students develop self-reliance are woven into the daily classroom routine. Youngsters who feel confident of their own abilities—both inside and outside the classroom—generally have a more positive attitude toward new experiences. That self-confidence will help them look forward eagerly to being on their own at home.

Often, lessons on self-reliance begin in kindergarten, with instruction on developing a positive self-image. The training results in a youngster who feels confident and capable. Hands-on units teach youngsters the basics of topics, such as using the telephone wisely, dealing with strangers, selectively choosing television programs, reacting correctly in case of a fire, handling peer pressure, and the importance of nutrition and exercise.

Through elementary school guidance counseling programs, all youngsters have an opportunity to share their concerns, as well as their successes, with one another. For instance, admitting a fear of storms is good for a latchkey kid as well as for the other children in the group who may not necessarily stay home alone. Sharing concerns provides an opportunity for discussion and group members realize they aren't the only ones frightened of storms.

If your school has self-help programs, either in the classroom or through the counseling program, ask the teacher or guidance counselor how what's being taught at school can be reinforced at home. For example, if your youngster is studying a unit on wise use of the telephone, let the child practice new skills at home. In mock phone conversations, assume the role of a stranger, a long-lost relative, or a salesperson and give your youngster the opportunity to react.

If the class is studying nutrition, let your youngster help integrate the new knowledge into her after-school snacks. If the curriculum revolves around fire safety, check your house for fire hazards with your youngster. If the group is discussing peer pressure, take on the role of a neighborhood child who is coaxing your youngster to ride her bicycle on a busy street.

Finally, encourage your child to talk with you about the class or small-group discussions. If you sense your youngster is having problems with self-confidence, talk to school personnel. It's much easier to deal with problems when the child is young, rather than waiting until the child is older and the problems are ingrained more firmly.

Getting into the Act

The subject of latchkey kids may be a hot topic, but it's not a new one. Latchkey arrangements have existed for years.

The difference today is that the issues of child welfare and child care have moved into the national limelight. Awareness of the needs of latchkey youngsters has grown. The list of organizations involved in improving the latchkey situation is long. Social welfare, educational, and public affairs organizations on the national, state, and local levels all provide information to help civic minded groups as well as individual families deal with the latchkey issues.

If you want more information about what's going on in your area, contact your school district, local college or university, community education department, or local and state organizations that concentrate on children's issues.

If your school district does not teach survival skills or offer confidence-building sessions, speak with your child's teacher or principal about adding such a curriculum. Also, discuss the possibility of your local parent-teacher association sponsoring a series of classes for the students. Suggest, too, that an adult education class be developed to help parents prepare their child for staying home alone.

Latchkey Learning Outside of School

Schools aren't the only entity fostering self-confidence and independence in youngsters. There are plenty of other organizations offering classes.

After-school classes. Many school districts offer community education classes in the school building after the regular school day is over. Most of these classes are optional, usually require a fee, and are geared to specific age levels.

Children's organizations. Camp Fire, Scouts, and other boys' and girls' organizations have incorporated units that teach children self-help skills. They include home safety, personal safety, and family responsibility. Most courses help youngsters cope with different life situations, including being alone before and after school.

To find the program that best suits your individual needs, ask these questions before making a choice:
- What are the program's basic lessons?
- How do class times fit into the family's schedule?
- Will transportation to or from the classes be a factor?
- What is the cost?
- Are the instructor's qualifications acceptable?
- Will any of my child's friends be in the class?
- Is this something my youngster will enjoy?
- Is my child already involved in a sufficient number of activities after school?

What Else Can You Do?

If you feel your youngster has outgrown the need for a baby-sitter or a day-care center, but you still do not feel comfortable leaving the child alone every day, there are some other options:
- Many elementary schools have before- and after-school programs. Unlike classes that help youngsters learn survival skills, these programs take the place of day-care and baby-sitters. Most offer activities, but also allow youngsters an opportunity to do homework, if they desire.
- Some employers offer flex-time schedules, so working parents can be home after school. Also, some couples or neighbors may alternate their hours so there's an adult available after school.
- If you feel your youngster is mature enough and seems interested, she could volunteer as an aide in a child-care facility, library, museum, or park program on a part-time basis. Volunteering will not only provide your youngster with a place to go after school, but also instill a sense of community service in her.

Keeping in Contact With Other Parents

Get to know the other parents in your neighborhood. They could be your best resources for assistance and vice versa. Consider:
- Sharing child transportation responsibilities. Arrange car pools according to everyone's work schedules or share the cost of a taxi. You'll worry less knowing your youngster is traveling with other neighborhood children.
- Making arrangements in case of unexpected events. Form a group of parents who are willing to share responsibilities among families. Then, if you find you won't be home until late at night, you can send your youngster to one of the other homes for supper and to spend the evening. Be available to return the favor.
- Talking periodically with the other parents. Share information about potentially dangerous situations, trade ideas about everything from snacks to after-school classes, and be assured you aren't the *only* parent in the world who won't let your youngster go to the mall every day after school is out.

INDEX

Especially for You

Deciding to Be A Latchkey Kid

What's a Latchkey Kid?

Do you have friends who are home alone every day before or after school? If so, you've probably heard them called "latchkey kids."

"Latchkey" is another way of saying "door key." People use the term "latchkey kids" when no adults are home. Latchkey kids let themselves in and take care of themselves until a parent gets home. That's a big responsibility.

Here are some hints for you if you're thinking about becoming a "latchkey kid."

Are You Ready?

There isn't one magical age when kids are ready to stay home alone. Kids younger than you already may be latchkey kids. Some of your older friends still may not stay home alone.

It's just like learning to ride a bicycle. Before you could ride a bike, you probably had a younger friend who already knew how. After you learned, you probably knew older kids who still couldn't ride a bike.

Chances are, if you're old enough to read and use this book, you're old enough to be a latchkey kid. Still, no matter what your age, it will be a big step. It's a sign that you are growing up.

Are Your Parents Ready?

Sometimes it's hard for parents to let their kids stay home alone. Maybe your folks don't feel you're mature enough to stay alone. They might think you can't handle the new responsibilities. If you're home alone, they might worry all the time.

You and your parents should talk over all these concerns.

Make a List

Here's how you and your folks can come to a decision about staying home alone.
● Write down all the good things about staying home by yourself. Maybe you want some quiet time to yourself. Perhaps you'd like to spend extra time with your dog or cat. Maybe you want time alone to read a good book or watch a special show on television.
● Now, write down the things that bother you about staying home alone. Are you afraid to answer the telephone? Are you worried that older brothers and sisters will pick on you?

• Ask Mom and Dad to make their own lists of pros and cons. You may be surprised at what you learn. Mom may be happy because she can talk to you on the telephone as soon as you get home from school, instead of waiting until suppertime. Perhaps Dad worries that you will be afraid to go into an empty house all by yourself.

Talk It Over

Once the lists are done, talk things over. Take one point from your list and discuss it. Then take one point from your parents' list and discuss it. Keep that up until you've covered everything.

Questions, Questions, Questions

Ask your folks lots of questions so they can help you figure out how to handle problems before they happen.

What can I eat?

Who can I call if I need help?

Can I watch TV?

Can I ask a friend over?

What should I do if a stranger comes to the front door?

What if my brother or sister keeps bugging me?

If I'm in an after-school activity, such as Scouting, can I still go?

If I take the school bus, what happens if I miss my ride?

The Big Decision

Be sure your family discusses all the good and not-so-good points about being a latchkey kid. Then, it's time to decide.

You and your parents may feel that you're ready to stay home alone. If so, read this book together. Then, make house rules. Be sure you agree with your parents on what each rule means.

If you and your parents decide you're not ready to stay home alone, that's OK. You shouldn't stay alone until both you *and* your parents are ready. Continue to go where you've been going before or after school. Then, in 6 months or so, talk again with your folks about staying home alone.

If You Change Your Mind

What if you stay home alone and don't like it? There's nothing wrong with that. People change their minds all the time.

Just tell Mom and Dad you don't like staying home alone and why. They will make other arrangements. Later, you may think you're ready to stay home alone. Then, talk about it with your Mom and Dad and try being a latchkey kid again.

Nuts and Bolts

Did you ever notice that life runs more smoothly when a parent is home?

If you can't find your tennis shoes, for example, Mom says, "They're by the chair in the family room." (Sure enough, they are!)

If you aren't getting along with friends or your brothers and sisters, Dad steps in and magically makes everyone feel good again.

When you're a latchkey kid, Mom or Dad won't always be around to handle problems, so you'll need to take on some new responsibilities.

Here are some hints to help you get along by yourself.

That's the Rule

Put together a list of rules with your parents' help. There are rules in this book that will help you get started. These "dos" and "don'ts" will help keep you safe.

Understanding the rules. Discuss each rule with your parents. Then, write down the ones that pertain to your family. Be sure you understand why each rule is necessary. Then, post your copy of the rules by the telephone or on the refrigerator. Then you can see it in a jiffy.

Breaking the rules. Talk about what happens if a rule is broken. Knowing the consequence ahead of time may keep you from breaking the rule in the first place.

Tour the House

Walk through the house with your folks. Take a pad of paper and a pencil and write down instructions. Here's what you should look for:

● Is there anything you shouldn't use when you're alone? Your parents' stereo system? A compact disc player? The kitchen stove? The food processor? Make a list of items you shouldn't use.

● What items do you need to know how to use when you're home alone? How about the telephone answering machine? Make a list of the items you need to learn to operate.

● Are there certain games or toys that will be off-limits when you have friends over and no adult is home? Write them down so you won't forget.

● Are there strange noises or dark corners in the house that bother you? Investigate them with your folks.

● Does your home have a burglar alarm or smoke detectors? Know what they sound like, and find out what you should do if they go off.

● Do your parents want the shades or curtains on first-floor windows closed while they're gone?

● If the house is too hot or too cold, can you adjust the thermostat? If so, learn how to work it.

● Where should you go to be safe if there's a bad storm?

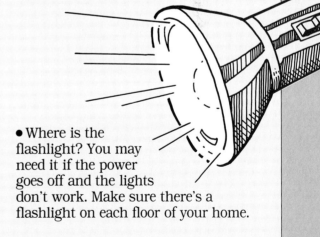

● Where is the flashlight? You may need it if the power goes off and the lights don't work. Make sure there's a flashlight on each floor of your home.

Stuff to Know

About the Key

- Practice using the key when your folks are around. Some keys work any way you put them in the keyhole. Others work only a certain way.

- If you have a front-door lock with push buttons on it, memorize the series of numbers.

- Don't hide the key outside the house. Instead, carry it with you or have a neighbor keep it.

- If your door has more than one lock and key, mark the key for the top lock with fingernail polish. Carry both keys on the same chain.

- If you carry the key, wear it on a string or chain around your neck or on a key chain attached to your belt. Keep the key hidden under your clothes or in your pants pocket during the day.

- If you can't get the key to turn, don't press so hard that you bend or break it. Instead, go to a neighbor's house for help unlocking the door.

- Have your folks leave an extra key with one or two neighbors. Then, if you lose your key, go to the neighbor's and get the extra one.

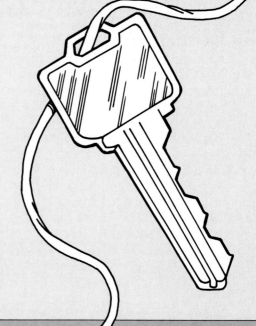

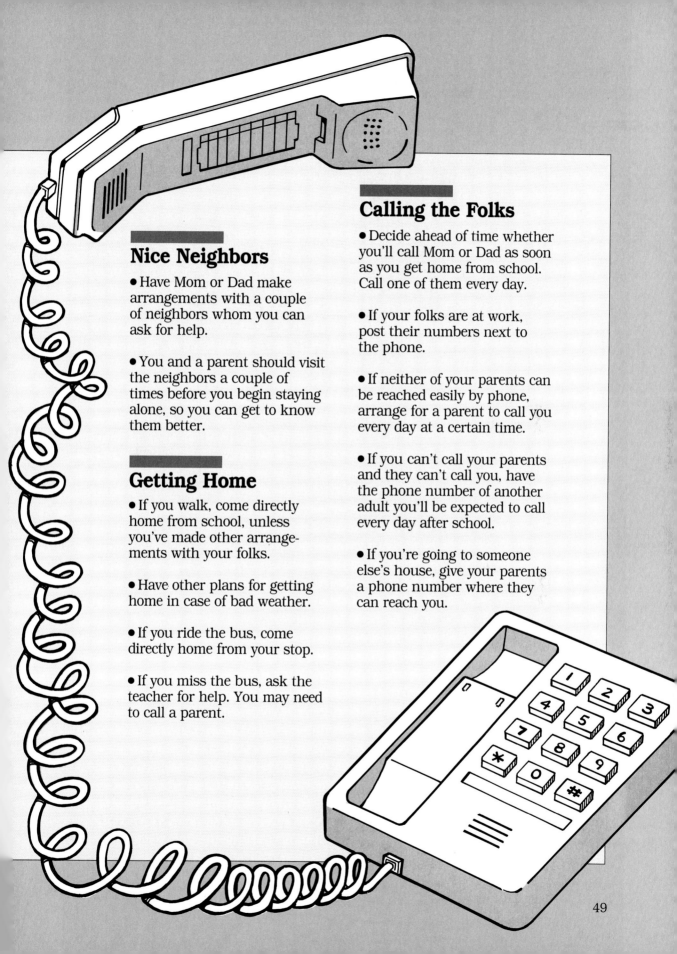

Nice Neighbors

• Have Mom or Dad make arrangements with a couple of neighbors whom you can ask for help.

• You and a parent should visit the neighbors a couple of times before you begin staying alone, so you can get to know them better.

Getting Home

• If you walk, come directly home from school, unless you've made other arrangements with your folks.

• Have other plans for getting home in case of bad weather.

• If you ride the bus, come directly home from your stop.

• If you miss the bus, ask the teacher for help. You may need to call a parent.

Calling the Folks

• Decide ahead of time whether you'll call Mom or Dad as soon as you get home from school. Call one of them every day.

• If your folks are at work, post their numbers next to the phone.

• If neither of your parents can be reached easily by phone, arrange for a parent to call you every day at a certain time.

• If you can't call your parents and they can't call you, have the phone number of another adult you'll be expected to call every day after school.

• If you're going to someone else's house, give your parents a phone number where they can reach you.

Rules of the House

Here are some very important subjects. They probably are ones you'll want to discuss with your folks as you're setting household rules. Think of the "dos" and "don'ts" of each topic. These rules you set are important because they will help you get along when you're home alone.

The Television

Watching television is one way to relax after school. But watching just anything or watching lots of television is not a good idea. Some adult programs could upset you instead of helping you relax. And there may be some shows on TV,

especially scary ones, that your folks don't want you to watch.

Here are some television guidelines:

- Decide with your parents which shows you should watch.

- Decide with your folks how much TV you should watch every day. Choose certain programs or set a time limit.

- Will you be at home with sisters and brothers? If so, decide with them the night before what programs to watch. If there's a disagreement, Mom or Dad can help settle it.

- Don't sit too close to the television set. It's hard on your eyes.

Instead of Television

Watching television isn't the only thing you can do after school. Lots of other activities are fun, too!

• Check out a crafts book from the library. The librarian can help you choose one that's right for you. Look through the book and pick out birthday presents you can make for members of your family. Be sure you have all the materials you'll need before you begin a project.

• Start a diary and write about your activities each day.

• Collect baseball cards, stamps, or coins. Hobby stores sell special books to use for displaying such collections.

• Cut out pictures of your favorite movie stars and paste them in a scrapbook.

• Read a good book—not for school—just for fun!

• Start your homework.

The Telephone

The telephone connects you with your parents and your friends. In case of an emergency, it's your link with the outside world. Even so, your parents probably won't want you to spend *all* your time talking on the phone. They might try to call you and wouldn't be able to get through.

Here are some hints for talking on the phone:

• Answer the phone by saying "Hello." Don't say your name.

• Always be polite to the caller. Don't scream or yell into the receiver.

• Keep a pad and pencil by the phone. If the call is not for you, write down a message.

• Never tell the caller you're home alone. Instead, say Mom or Dad can't come to the phone right now. Tell the caller your parent will return the call soon.

• If you get a prank phone call, don't say anything. Instead, hang up and tell your folks when they get home. If you get a lot of scary calls, call a parent. You can also go to a neighbor's house until an adult gets home.

Playing Outside

Some parents like their youngsters to stay indoors when adults aren't there. If your parents allow you to be outside, know your boundaries. Are they the yard? The block? Make sure you and your parents have the same set of boundaries in mind.

When you play outside:
- Change into play clothes *first!*
- If you lock the house, take the key with you.
- Ask beforehand whether you can have friends over. If you can, how many may you invite?
- Decide beforehand if friends can go inside for a drink or to use the bathroom.
- Know where you'll go for help if someone gets hurt.

Riding a bicycle.
Will you be allowed to ride a bike when you're alone? How far may you go? Stay away from busy streets and intersections. Use your hand signals. Never "ride double." And wear a helmet.

Swimming pool. If you have a swimming pool, *never* swim when your parents aren't home, even if you're a good swimmer.

I'M TELLING MOM!

Getting Along with Brothers and Sisters

If you will be home with brothers and sisters, ask your family to set rules ahead of time.

Here are some suggestions:

• Decide if each of you has certain responsibilities or if one person is in charge. A lot depends upon your ages.

• Pick a place in the house that's a "neutral spot." If there's a fight, each of you can go to your own neutral spot to be alone for a while.

• If you and your brothers and sisters can't settle a fight, wait until Mom or Dad gets home to discuss it.

• If it looks like someone will get hurt or something will get broken, call a parent. Mom or Dad can't do much over the phone, except get tempers settled until they get home.

• Learn the difference between "tattling" (which nobody likes) and "informing." If your sister or brother should be picking up toys, but is watching television instead, it's probably "tattling" to tell your folks. If your sister or brother should be picking up toys, but instead is riding a bicycle on a busy street, telling your parents is "informing." Whenever a brother or sister is in danger, your folks need to know.

Having Friends Over

You sometimes may want friends to come over to play after school. Talk about it with your folks. How old you are and how close your friends live will make a difference.

Planning will mean fewer problems and more time for play. Here are points to think about:

• Make plans the night before a friend is to come over. Be sure your friend's parents know your parents won't be home after school.

• If you ride the bus or are in a carpool, how will your friend get to your house?

• Ask your folks what toys or games are off-limits when they aren't home.

• If you and your friend have difficulty getting along, your friend probably should go home. If that isn't possible, play a different game, or watch television for a while. If that still doesn't work, ask a neighbor for help.

The Kitchen

How much you can do in the kitchen depends on how old you are.

Snacking. Decide with your folks on snacks for after school. Granola bars, fresh fruit, or yogurt don't take any preparation.

Do you like to make things in the kitchen? Make a plate of cheese and crackers, or toast a bagel or English muffin and spread it with peanut butter or jam. Or, make a smiley face on a round cracker. Just spread peanut butter on the cracker, and use raisins for the eyes and mouth.

No matter what you make, remember: Clean up after yourself. Also, don't fill up on snacks, or you won't be hungry for dinner.

Using appliances. Depending on how old you are, some appliances will be off-limits. Fancy food processors often come with complicated instructions and sharp blades. Hot ovens or stove tops, too, may be more than you should handle.

On the other hand, most kids can use a microwave oven. And every kid knows how to raid the refrigerator!

Talk to your parents about kitchen appliances. Decide which ones you can and cannot use. As you get older, you'll be able to use more and more appliances.

Remember these important safety rules in the kitchen:
- Unplug the electric mixer before you put in or take out the beaters.
- Keep your wet hands away from appliances and electrical outlets.
- Leave sharp knives alone.
- Wipe up spills immediately.

Starting supper. You can really help Mom and Dad by starting supper. Begin by making a tossed salad or setting the table. As you get older, ask to share in the menu planning. Pick out parts of the meal you can prepare. Try simple items such as canned soup, grilled cheese sandwiches, and a gelatin salad. For dessert, bake a cake in the microwave oven.

Cleaning up. No matter what you make, be sure to:
- Rinse dishes and put them in the dishwasher or stack them neatly in the sink.
- Wipe off the counter.
- Wrap or cover leftover food and put it away.

The Chores

Ignoring chores won't make them go away, so:
- Make a daily list of household chores ahead of time. Check off each one as you finish it.
- If you have a lot of homework, do some before supper.
- If you have a pet, take care of it as soon as you get home from school. If it's a dog or cat, spend some time with it. Pets like attention.

• If you play a musical instrument, practice part of your lesson before supper.

• As you get older, you'll have more and more after-school chores. To get everything done and still have some fun, ask Mom or Dad to help you make out a schedule. For example, give yourself from 3:30 to 4 p.m. to play with the dog. From 4 to 4:30, practice piano. From 4:30 to 5, watch television or read a good book, and so on.

Safe and Secure

Before you begin staying alone, talk about safety with your folks. For example, rehearse what to do in case a stranger comes to the door. Also, learn what to do in case someone gets hurt.

First Aid

Put together a first-aid kit. Then practice first-aid measures with Mom or Dad before you stay home alone. (See pages 63 and 64 for first-aid tips.) Then, if you get a small cut or scrape, a little burn, or a nosebleed, you can take care of yourself. If anything bigger happens, call a neighbor.

Here's what you should put in the kit:
● A cotton washcloth for cleaning cuts;
● A box of different sized bandages for small cuts and scrapes;
● Gauze pads and adhesive tape to cover large cuts;
● A small pair of scissors to cut the tape;
● An elastic bandage for use on a sprain;
● Calamine lotion for insect bites;
● A bottle of aspirin substitute for headaches;
● Tweezers for removing slivers;
● An antibiotic ointment for minor scrapes or cuts;
● Temperature strips. (Ask Mom or Dad to teach you how to use them.)

Also, keep an ice pack in the freezer. Or, know where plastic bags are kept, so you can fill one with ice.

In Case of Fire

Your family should practice two plans of escape from each area of the house. In case of a fire, use those same routes, even if you are home alone. Go immediately to a neighbor's to call the

FIRST-AID
GERM BUSTERS

HELP!

Some problems aren't emergencies. Still, they are problems that probably cannot wait until Mom or Dad gets home. Whenever you are in doubt about a problem, it is best if you call a parent.

If you can't reach a parent, call a neighbor.

Some problems are definitely emergencies. These include situations such as a fire, someone choking, a cut that won't stop bleeding, swallowing poison, or a person who is in a lot of pain.

In case of an emergency, call for professional help before you call anyone else.

If your community has a 911 emergency number, call that number no matter what the emergency is. The person answering your call has been trained to help and will give you instructions immediately.

If your community doesn't have 911, dial 0. Ask the operator for help. Then, follow the operator's directions exactly. Finally, call your parents or a neighbor.

fire department or the emergency number. Then, call your parents.

If you are home with brothers and sisters, know where everyone will meet once they've left the house. Once you're together, know who will be responsible for calling the fire department or the emergency number, as well as contacting your parents.

Extra Change

Hide some coins outside your home. You may need the "emergency change" if you get locked out and your neighbors aren't home. Use the money to call your folks from a pay telephone or to take a bus or a taxi.

Taking Medicine

Don't take any medicine unless you have a parent's permission.

If you're taking medicine that was ordered by your doctor, have Mom or Dad measure and mark the correct amount. Never take more than that. Never take medicine that's been prescribed for another member of your family.

Use Me!!

Fill out the next 3 pages of this book. Then, cut each page out along the dotted lines and have one of your parents laminate them. Keep the pages in a handy place—maybe on the bulletin board or the refrigerator. Then, you can use them when you need them.

Read this page first. It will tell you how the information on those pages can help you when you're home alone.

Telephone Numbers

Ask a parent to help you fill in the telephone numbers you'll need when you're home alone. Keep this list on the bulletin board or in a drawer next to your phone. Post a list of emergency numbers by every telephone in your home.

Ask your parents if your phone has memory buttons. On some phones, you can call certain people by punching a memory button and one other number. On other phones, you only need to punch a single button. If your phone has a memory, learn how to use it. Write down which numbers or buttons you use to call your parents, a neighbor, or your special friend.

Safety Rules

Carefully talk about each safety rule with your folks. If you don't understand a certain rule, be sure to ask about it.

First-Aid Rules

Read and discuss each rule with your parents. Any time you're not sure how to handle a first-aid situation, call for help. ***Never try to give first aid when you are not sure what to do!***

Names and Phone Numbers of Family and Friends

Mom at work: _____

Dad at work: _____

A special neighbor: _____

Another special neighbor: _____

My grandma and grandpa: _____

My other grandma and grandpa: _____

My favorite aunt or uncle: _____

My friends _____

_____

_____

_____

_____

_____

_____

_____

Telephone Numbers in Case of Emergency

Emergency number: _____

Fire Department: _____

Police Department: _____

My doctor: _____

Ambulance: _____

Poison Control Center: _____

Other Names and Numbers

The library: _____

Homework hotline: _____

My school: _____

My music teacher: _____

My coach: _____

Special help (such as Phone Friend, Kids' Line): _____

_____

Others: _____

Safety Rules

In Your Home

- Lock the door after you get inside.
- If a stranger—even a delivery person or a police officer—comes to the door, don't answer. If it's important, that person will come back later.
- If you live in an apartment building with an intercom system and someone buzzes you, don't answer it. If it's important, the caller will return.
- If you get home from school and the door already is open, don't go in unless you know that your parents are home early. Also, if any windows are open that were closed when you left, go to a neighbor's and call your parents or the police.

In Case of Fire

- *Get out immediately.*
- Run to a neighbor's house or to a nearby telephone. Dial 911 or 0 for help *before* you call to alert your parents.
- Do not go back in the house for anything—even a pet.

In Case of a Tornado

- If bad weather is approaching, listen to the radio or television. The announcer may say there is a **watch** (which means to be on the alert for more information about a possible storm). Or there may be a **warning** (which means a storm or tornado actually has been sighted). In case of a warning, take shelter immediately.
- Likewise, if you hear a weather siren outside, take cover.
- If you have a basement, go there. Lie flat on the floor or crouch under a piece of heavy furniture, like a work table.
- If you don't have a basement, lie flat on the lowest floor in your house or apartment building.
- Don't get back up until you hear an all-clear signal or your parent or an adult arrives.

If You Smell Gas

- Leave the house immediately.
- Run to a neighbor's house and call 911 or 0 and tell the person that you smell gas.
- Then, call your parents.

Overflowing Toilet

- Turn the wheel or knob by the bottom of the toilet to shut the water off.
- Mop up the water on the floor.
- Don't try to fix the toilet. Wait for a parent to come home.

It's Broken!

Windows. With shoes on, sweep broken glass into a corner. If the weather's bad, *very carefully* tape a piece of cardboard over the broken window. Let Mom or Dad pick up the glass and fix the window.

Appliances. If you already know how to operate an appliance and it doesn't work the way it should, use dry hands to unplug it. Wait for a parent to come home. Don't try to fix the appliance yourself.

Special toys. Don't call a parent. Your folks can't fix your toys over the telephone, but they'll deal with them when they get home.

TURN KNOB

First-Aid Rules

Small Cuts

- Hold the cut or scrape under running water or sponge it with soap and water, and a clean washcloth, tissue, or paper towel. If the cut is bleeding a lot, gently press the washcloth against the cut until the bleeding stops.
- When the bleeding stops, put an adhesive bandage on the cut to keep it clean.
- If the cut has not stopped bleeding within 5 minutes, call a neighbor.

Large Cuts

- Sponge the cut with soap and water, and a large, clean cloth (perhaps a hand towel).
- Put a gauze pad on the cut and hold it there firmly to stop the bleeding. At the same time, lift the injury higher than your chest, if possible.
- If the blood is gushing or squirting and doesn't stop, hold the gauze pad in place while you dial 911 or 0.
- Don't put antiseptics or ointment on the wound without medical advice from an adult.

Small Burns

- Put the burn in cold water for 2 or 3 minutes. Or, hold an ice cube or ice pack on it until it stops hurting.
- Carefully dry the burn with a clean towel.
- Gently cover the area with a bandage or gauze pad and tape it in place.
- Call a parent.

Large Burns

- If the burn is big, or looks white or charred, immediately dial 911 or 0. Or call an ambulance.
- Cover the area with a clean sheet.
- If the burn is on your arm or leg, raise the arm or leg higher than your chest.

Nosebleeds

- Do not lie down. Instead, sit quietly for 5 minutes with your nose pinched shut.
- If the bleeding doesn't stop, put an ice pack or bag of ice against your nose.
- If it doesn't stop, call a parent.

Poison

- If you drink something you think is poisonous, drink two glasses of milk right away.
- Save the container that the poison was in.
- Dial 911 or 0 or call the Poison Control Center *immediately.*

Unconsciousness

- Do not move the unconscious person! Instead, dial 911 or 0 and follow directions.

Choking

- Try to cough up or swallow the object.
- If that doesn't work, make a double fist with your hands, then push in and up between your waist and rib cage. Or push your stomach against something hard.
- If that doesn't work, dial 911 or 0 immediately.

Sprains

- If you've hurt your ankle, wrist, finger, or knee, watch for swelling. You might have a sprain.
- Place an ice pack or a plastic bag filled with ice on the sprain for at least 15 minutes.
- Wrap the sprain with an elastic bandage.
- Call a parent. (The sprain might actually be a broken bone.)

Broken Bones

- Don't move a bone that you think is broken.
- Remove any tight clothing or shoes from around the injury.
- Dial 911 or 0.